THE ANGER CURE

A Step-by-Step Program to Reduce Anger, Rage, Negativity, Violence, and Depression in Your Life

Kathleen O'Bannon, C.N.C.

Basic Health
PUBLICATIONS, INC.

The information contained in this book is based upon the research and personal and professional experiences of the author. It is not intended as a substitute for consulting with your physician or other healthcare provider. Any attempt to diagnose and treat an illness should be done under the direction of a healthcare professional.

The publisher does not advocate the use of any particular healthcare protocol but believes the information in this book should be available to the public. The publisher and author are not responsible for any adverse effects or consequences resulting from the use of the suggestions, preparations, or procedures discussed in this book. Should the reader have any questions concerning the appropriateness of any procedures or preparation mentioned, the author and the publisher strongly suggest consulting a professional healthcare advisor.

The names and/or circumstances of the people in the quotes have been changed to protect the privacy of Kathleen O'Bannon's friends and clients.

Basic Health Publications, Inc.
28812 Top of the World Drive
Laguna Beach, CA 92651
949-715-7327 • www.basichealthpub.com

O'Bannon, Kathleen.
    The anger cure : a step-by-step program to reduce anger, rage,
negativity, violence, and depression in your life / Kathleen O'Bannon
        p. cm.
    Includes bibliographical references and index.
    ISBN 978-1-59120-199-1
    1. Anger. 2. Anger—Treatment. I. Title.

    RC569.5.A53O23   2007
    616.85'2—dc22

                                    2007006950

Editor: Susan Davis
Typesetting/Book design: Gary A. Rosenberg
Cover design: Mike Stromberg

Printed in the United States of America

10   9   8   7   6   5   4   3   2   1

Contents

Acknowledgments

This book would not have been possible without the input of all the people who over the years asked me to help them overcome anger in their lives. A lot of them didn't know that anger was their main problem, but when they were rid of it, they were glad. So thank you to all the people I have worked with in nutrition programs in clinics, private practice, or classes in the United States and Canada.

I would also like to thank all the people who have encouraged me to do this book and stick with it: the late Phil Gilliam, who bugged me almost daily to do this work; Marianne Woodson, O.B.J.N., a fabulous spiritual director, who hounded me with questions and research that were so important for this book; Charlie Fox, Mr. Garlic, who began every conversation for a year with "How's the book coming?" and introduced me to Norman Goldfind, my publisher; Charlene Green, my friend of so many years I don't even want to put dates on paper, who encouraged me to do this book because she believes people need to hear this information and that I'm the one to relay it to them, who lectures me all the time on business, investing, and other things I couldn't imagine understanding or knowing, but she makes it so easy, I finally have understood it; and Dave Lampi, an old friend from high school, who sent me cards and e-mails of encouragement to make sure I finished this book.

This book would not be in order and read so smoothly without all the fabulous work my editor, Susan E. Davis, did on the manuscript. We laughed over some of my bad grammar habits that showed up over and over, while she gently insisted on correcting them. I also want to thank my sister, Carole Eisenlord, for giving me moral and emotional support throughout all the writing, editing, and recipe making. Most of all I want to thank Jim Weismann of Carson City, Nevada, who did the graphics and artwork. Without him this book might be dull and boring.

Foreword

With this book, Kathleen O'Bannon has forged a *gold standard* in the field of nutrition and health education, especially as that relates to anger. As if she were a conductor of a fine symphony, she has brought together a wonderful harmony of information and guidance across a broad range of disciplines and practices. The resulting composition is one from which we are able to fashion a *life-dance* that transcends anger and imbalance in our lives while deftly moving us toward vitality, longevity, and peace.

As a licensed clinical psychologist who has worked very extensively and over many years with anger-problem patients, I can attest that the step-by-step program designed by Kathleen is practical and comprehensive. Accordingly, its broad application to one's overall health and quality of life may indeed be unprecedented. The scope of this particular work, along with its pragmatic and highly interdisciplinary perspective, represents a quantum leap forward in our understanding. This work may well become the *seminal piece* for a new era of understanding about health practices, nutrition, and anger. This work is a *great resource* for health professionals and laypersons alike.

A substantive and truly profound work, this book establishes Kathleen as a nutrition and health expert with few contemporaries. She writes clearly and brilliantly on how we can use diet, supplements, and lifestyle changes to improve our health. As one of the vanguard researchers in this field, Kathleen has amassed more than thirty years of experience in health and nutrition work. Over this time she has continuously evolved, tediously integrating the latest and most up-to-date practices and information as such became available.

I am deeply honored to write this foreword. Even more so, I am excited about the potential for great good to flourish in the lives of those who heed the guidelines, advice, and practices presented in this work. I invite you, I encourage you, I beseech you to make this book—truly a gift to humankind!—a part of your daily reading.

Eke F. Wokocha, Ph.D., Licensed Clinical Psychologist
Alafia Wellness Center, Lemon Grove, California

Introduction

This book shows you the nutritional way to overcome anger and all its variations: rage, violence, fatigue, anxiety, temper tantrums, allergies, lack of sex drive, insomnia, low self-esteem, and eventually, if ignored, its physiological manifestation in diabetes, heart disease, cancer, arthritis, obesity, addictions, and premature aging. You will also learn how to free yourself of anger and hate and become more loving. When you begin to deal with life through your heart instead of your liver and adrenals, you will automatically be more loving. To me, anger is the opposite of love.

Originally I called this health system "The Love Diet" because when you have what I call the "anger syndrome," you shut down your physical and emotional heart and can't love. This has been called "hardness of heart" for thousands of years. It's well recorded in the Hebrew Bible that people hardened their hearts when they didn't want to face something. In these times the standard American diet (SAD) does a much better, faster job of shutting down or hardening your heart.

VICTIMS

Your body, mind, and spirit are victims of your lifestyle. If you provide the fuel for your body to be healthy, you will not have anger, rage, or violence. You *will* be loving. If you provide the fuel that causes damage to your body and mind, you will reap the consequences. And if you go to extremes with SAD, you can destroy your spirit and conscience; you won't be able to tell right from wrong.

IT'S NOT YOUR FAULT

This is probably the first time you've ever been told that if you have an anger problem, no matter how small or how large, it's not your fault. It is not your fault! However, once you read this book, it will be your fault if you continue to pursue the lifestyle that contributes to your anger. You will now have within your control all the answers to why you have anger and angry outbursts. It's up to you to do something about it.

ANGER AND RAGE

Here are some dictionary definitions of anger: A strong feeling of displeasure or hostility. A strong passion or emotion of displeasure or antagonism, excited by a real or supposed injury or insult to one's self or others, or by the intent to do such injury. A feeling of keen displeasure (usually with a desire to punish) for what we regard as wrong toward ourselves or others; it may be excessive or misplaced, but is not necessarily criminal. A feeling that is oriented toward some real or supposed grievance. Belligerence aroused by a real or supposed wrong.

Here are some dictionary definitions of rage: Violent, explosive anger; a fit of anger; furious intensity, as of a storm or disease; a burning desire; a passion. To speak or act in violent anger; to be furious with anger; to be exasperated to fury. To be violently agitated with passion; to be violent and tumultuous; to be violently driven or agitated; to act or move furiously.

To me, anger is turning that emotion in on yourself and rage is turning that emotion outward to others. Anger doesn't necessarily have to be a big emotion. Anger can be something as simple as the emotion you feel and direct toward yourself when the car in front of you at the light suddenly turns on its left-turn signal just as the light changes and you have to wait. You had already checked the car out and chose to stay behind it because it was not turning. So you get angry with yourself for making the wrong choice and angry with the person for not signaling soon enough so you could avoid the wait. In the process you have produced the chemical cortisol in your body that can cause damage. If these little episodes of anger continue, you may eventually exhibit rage at the person by yelling or gesturing at the driver of the car. Because I view anger and rage as different expressions of the same emotion, I use both terms throughout the book. But for simplicity's sake I chose to focus on anger in the title.

IS THIS YOU?

Can you relate to any of the definitions of anger and rage? They really describe the way a lot of people act every day, often several times a day. It is especially interesting to me that anger can be triggered by a real or supposed injury or insult. That is exactly what happens when your body is out of chemical balance. The slightest event appears to be an injury.

When you are hurrying to get to work and your little one spills milk, it appears to be an injury to you and causes you to become angry. But is it really? No. The chances are great that your little one couldn't move as fast as you could and accidentally spilled the milk. It's not an injury to you. If you took it as one and lashed out at your child, you have an anger problem.

Often parents have anger because they expect their children to be able to do more than the children physically can. And when they drop something or make a mess because their little hands or brains are not developed enough to accomplish the task, you get angry with them. You might even fly into a rage. All because you are out of balance in your body.

Exhibiting anger and rage are actually choices you make when you allow your body to control you instead of you controlling your body. *The Anger Cure* will describe the lifestyles and habits that you use to allow your body to be out of your control so you can have anger and rage. The goal of the Anger Cure program is to help you learn how to become more in balance and, therefore, less angry and less filled with rage.

Many people enjoy rage. Do you? Even if you want to stop, you can't because it gives you an adrenaline boost or a rush more powerful than caffeine. But when you follow the Anger Cure, you won't need the adrenaline boost from a rage attack. Many rage-a-holics become insulin-dependent diabetics because they have exhausted (fatigued) their body. Are you headed for that?

SYNDROME X

Syndrome X (also called metabolic syndrome, hyperinsulinism, or insulin resistance) is the latest disease produced by SAD and various lifestyle choices that cause anger and rage to emerge. People in North America experience anger, depression, anxiety, and rage in epidemic proportions. But you can do something about it. You can choose to take control of your actions and reactions to life. The chemistry of your body is in your hands.

TAKE THE TESTS

Just take the tests at the beginning of the first few chapters and you can determine if this program is for you. In my nearly thirty years of planning diet and lifestyle programs for people, I have found these tests to give an accurate picture of the ways your metabolism is causing anger, rage, violence, and a lot of other behavior problems that can be changed. You can learn to not have anger and to love. Even if your parents and grandparents had these same poor nutrition and lifestyle habits, you can become aware of them and change them with little effort.

PSYCHIATRIC HELP

Many psychological problems can be traced to Syndrome X, blood sugar fluctuations, low nutrients in your body, yeast overgrowth, and a lot of other health problems you will understand better once you have read this book. This doesn't mean you can eliminate your medication or give up your psychiatrist or psychologist. Please enlist the help of any counselors you are seeing. Tell them what you are doing so they can decrease your medications as you gain control of your energy and mood fluctuations. Many patients in clinics where I have worked have gone off high doses of psychotropic or psychoactive drugs by following this plan. However, I cannot stress strongly enough: *Please do not alter any dosage you are on without your doctor's consent.*

If you truly have an emotional problem, it will be a lot easier to deal with when you are no longer reacting to every little external trigger because you have eliminated the physiological reasons for anger and rage.

DRUGS

When you think of your food as your medicine, you will no longer need most mood-altering prescription or street drugs to take the place of proper nutrition and to lead to dynamic health. It is a slow process. For every year you have mistreated your body with poor lifestyle choices, it might take you at least one month to notice recovery. If you have had the anger problem for ten years, you can expect it will take about ten months to feel better. Some people notice headaches disappearing in three days; for others it takes weeks. There may be days you feel rotten and days you feel great. Gradually, you will feel better and better until you don't have any down or rotten days. You deserve to feel good all the time. You never deserve to have a bad day.

CHEMICAL IMBALANCE

Yes, there is such a thing as a "chemical imbalance," but it can be corrected when you learn how to do it. Drugs do not reverse chemical imbalances; they cover them up. When you understand that poor eating and drinking habits can lead to a chemical imbalance, you can begin to be healthy and drug-free. Anger and rage will no longer be part of your life. If you don't believe me, just try the Anger Cure for six months. You will cure your anger responses and open your heart to love. You owe it to yourself and your family to follow the Anger Cure.

HOW IT ALL WORKS

Each chapter covers a specific subject. Each chapter progresses to the next, so it's important to read through the book and take the tests and then go back to study or review a particular topic.

Chapter 1, Go to the Mirror: It Doesn't Lie, looks at B complex vitamins and how you can tell by looking at your tongue, lips, and hands which B vitamins you need and why. This is important because it shows how all beauty problems like wrinkles, brown spots, and cracks are actually just signs of B complex vitamin deficiencies and that some emotional problems like a quick temper, might be related to B vitamin deficiencies.

Chapter 2, The Hidden Killer of Relationships and Love, focuses on the major health problem that can be almost solely responsible for anger, rage, and a host of other negative reactions that lead to angry outbursts and violence. You might be surprised that some other symptoms you thought you just had to live with can also be solved with proper lifestyle.

Chapter 3, Lips Together/Teeth Apart, is a break from nutrition and deals with relaxation through breathing and stress management using body, jaw, and tongue exercises.

Chapter 4, Chew On This, picks up from Chapter 2 and shows how stress stops digestion and what the outcome of this can mean for anger, digestion, and nutrient breakdown and absorption. We discuss the nutrients essential for relaxation and peace.

Chapter 5, Are You Hardening Your Heart?, delves deeper into blood sugar and heart problems, also called metabolic syndrome or Syndrome X. Although this may be a new way for you to look at blood sugar imbalances, it is not new to holistic health practitioners. It shows how blood sugar dysregulation and fluctuations can cause the problems that lead to anger and heart disease.

Chapter 6, Your Expanding Universe, details how yeast overgrowth in your body can be directly related to anger. Everything you need to know to overcome a yeast problem is spelled out in this chapter.

Chapter 7, How Your Body Creates Anger, discusses the organs in your body that relate to anger, including the liver (the seat of anger in Chinese medicine) and the adrenals. The discussion is purposefully not very scientific so it's easy to understand.

Chapter 8, Anger and the Fight-or-Flight Response, describes in detail the lifestyles, food, stinking thinking, and other habits that lead to anger and rage. And it gives the solutions you need to overcome fight-or-flight reactions in your life.

Chapter 9, What Throws You Off, is a simple-to-understand exposé of the twenty-two lifestyle errors that might be responsible for anger and rage in your life. There is even a way to do your own detective work to find out which ones are actually affecting you. I call this the Diet and Lifestyle Log and have used it for close to thirty years. Now you will have the personal lifestyle counseling that I have used to help people gain control of their health and life.

Chapter 10, The Anger Cure Program, is the actual diet and discussion of the Anger Cure program.

Chapter 11, The Body/Mind Connection, gives specific exercises for using relaxation and forgiveness to release anger and rage from your body and mind.

ARE YOU READY TO BE FREE OF ANGER?

Now is the time to decide if you are ready to be free of anger and rage. First, you must admit that you have anger—no matter how inconsequential it seems to you. Then you need to take the step of reading this book and following the suggestions, no matter how stupid you might feel they are. Eventually, you will be healthier and free of anger. An old saying is appropriate here: A net is only as strong as its weakest link. Each time you begin to improve your health and life, you will be influencing others to do the same. You can become the strongest link instead of the weakest. You will surely want to help your family by helping yourself. Don't pass on your weaknesses. Become the strongest link.

CHAPTER 1

Go to the Mirror:
It Doesn't Lie

"I don't know what to do, Kathleen. I'm tired all the time; I have to take a nap every day when I get home from work. Some weekends are a total loss because I sleep through them. I can't sleep at night. I have migraines. My stomach hurts all the time even though I take drugs for it. I'm gaining weight. Why, I'm over three hundred pounds and I'm only five feet tall. My asthma and allergies are so bad I might have to quit work. I keep flying off the handle at people, and it surprises them and me. I just don't know what to do."

Mary was desperate. Her doctor didn't know what to do for her. This is the kind of story I hear all the time. People who ache, feel bad, have allergies, have problems with anger or rage, and/or are depressed often suffer from all kinds of illnesses or health problems that they can't seem to find help for. Many times they're taking prescription drugs and aren't getting any better. In fact, they're getting worse.

Has this ever happened to you? Do you feel really great all the time, or do you wish you could feel better? Do you suffer from allergies, headaches, colds, viruses, stomachaches, depression, stiff and sore muscles, anger, rage, or any number of health problems that you just can't seem to get help with or get over?

Worse yet, have you gotten so used to feeling under the weather that you don't even think about it anymore? If you can relate to any of this, then this book is for you!

START AT THE BEGINNING

First read this book from the beginning to the end. Then go back and pick at it. Once you've gone through it, you can select what to reread.

The first essential is to be honest with yourself. Before you answer the various health questionnaires, please read over all the questions and pay close attention to yourself for days. Don't absentmindedly scratch your head and then write down that you never itch. Be aware of what you are doing for the next few days so you can answer the questions accurately.

START SIMPLE: LOOK IN A MIRROR

Look in a big mirror that's well lit. I suggest the bathroom mirror. Keep your face relaxed and gently stick out your tongue. Keep your tongue relaxed so that it's not pointy or strained. Take a good look! What do you see? A normal tongue. I'll bet not.

Is the tip shiny red? Does it look like a strawberry? Is it pale or light pink? Are the sides scalloped? Is there a coating of white or black on your tongue? (I once had a schizophrenic client who had a black tongue.) Does it have a deep ridge in the middle? Are there little patches of stuff that look like the center of an artichoke? These are all signs of nutritional deficiencies. Look at Table 1.1 to see which symptoms apply to your tongue.

Tongues Can Change

Many deficiencies show up on your tongue. The sad news is that when your doctor looks at your tongue, he or she isn't looking for nutritional deficiencies. The doctor is just looking to see if you have a mouth or throat problem. It's too bad because many diseases can be nipped in the bud by recognizing nutritional deficiencies—no matter what the cause—and changing your diet or adding a supplement. Mind you, it's not your doctor's fault that that wasn't taught in medical school. Only in the last twenty years has there been an increased interest in nutrition among doctors and medical schools, thanks to the tireless efforts of other practitioners who promote health and wellness.

Many deficiencies show up on your tongue.

TABLE 1.1. STORIES THE TONGUE CAN TELL	
TONGUE SIGN	**WHAT IT MEANS**
Enlarged bumps on front	B vitamin deficiency
Enlarged bumps on sides	B vitamin deficiency
Enlarged bumps on back	B vitamin deficiency
Smooth tip or sides	B vitamin deficiency
Groves in tongue	B vitamin deficiency
Grove in center	Allergies, spine out of alignment
Coated	Poor digestion, lack of good bacteria
Coated, fuzzy	B vitamin deficiency, poor digestion
Tip smooth, shiny, bright red	B_{12} deficiency
Scallops on sides	B_5 deficiency
Canker sores	B_3 deficiency
Enlarged, beefy	B_5 deficiency
Magenta color	B_2 deficiency
Strawberry color	B_{12} and folic acid deficiency
Tip very red, size wrong, coated	B_3 deficiency
Sore	B_6 deficiency
Sore	B vitamin deficiency
Sore	Too much sugar
Any of these symptoms	Anemia, poor digestion, low B vitamins

Note: Never take individual B vitamins unless under the care of a nutritionist or nutritionally oriented doctor. Always take a complete B complex. It will contain at least eleven nutrients if it is complete.

If you look at your tongue over a period of six months or a year, you might see changes as you undergo different stresses in your life or eat different foods. In the summer you might eat more raw vegetables and fruits, and you will see the coating diminish. Raw fruits and vegetables contain more enzymes that help with digestion than cooked foods. Raw foods also contain more vitamins and minerals than most cooked foods. You might take more time to exercise or relax in the summer so your digestion improves. There are so many variables. That's why the Anger Cure is so helpful. You will be able to chart your own lifestyle needs and adjust them to your body for each season, stress level, and amount of activity.

Tongue Cleaning

Did you know that the tongue is an organ of elimination and needs to be cleaned daily just the same as your teeth? When you brush your teeth in the morning and evening, it's essential to clean your tongue with a tongue cleaner or scraper. You can use the bowl of a teaspoon or a specialized tongue scraper. Dentists often have plastic tongue scrapers they give to patients, and many health food stores sell them. The one I use came from India and is stainless steel, but the one my dentist gave me is plastic. Either will do.

First, wet the tongue cleaner, and starting at the back of the tongue, drag it forward, scraping off any debris that accumulates there. This waste material (it might even be toxic) needs to be removed and discarded. Clean the scraper after each use and then continue several more times until the scraper is clean when you draw it across the tongue. Rinse the scraper thoroughly and put it away clean just like you would your toothbrush. Scraping your tongue will help prevent sinus infections, colds, and all kinds of health conditions that can come from bacteria living in the debris near the back of your throat.

Mothers Love Tongues

When I was a child, my mother never tired of asking me to stick out my tongue. She always said the same thing, "Just as I thought, constipated." Then she made me drink some really terrible, salty, fizzy stuff that was supposed to help if I could get it to stay down long enough. If only we had eaten whole-grain bread, I might not have had this problem. If she had known about the nutrition in the Anger Cure, I wouldn't have been made to drink that stuff!

Did your mother look at your tongue? Did she know what it meant? By the end of this book, you'll know everything about how your body functions and why. Isn't that fantastic!

GO TO THE MIRROR AGAIN

Look in the mirror again. This time look at your lips. What do you see? Do you have cracks in the corners? Does it look like you're whistling when you're not? Are they chapped or shredded? All of these symptoms are related

If you don't get the correct amount of B vitamins at the correct time, you will exhibit many of these symptoms chronically.

to B complex vitamin deficiency. If you don't get the correct amount of B vitamins at the correct time, you will exhibit many of these symptoms chronically. If your digestion is poor and you can't breakdown and/or absorb the nutrients in your food or supplements, you will also have many of these symptoms. B complex vitamins—there are a lot of them—are also helpful in reducing stress reactions. If you are under a lot of stress, you will need a lot more B vitamins than a person not under stress.

And you thought these symptoms just happened? Well, very little just happens in your body; most of it is related to some nutrient that is missing from your diet or is not digested. Look at Table 1.2 and see which symptoms apply to your lips.

TABLE 1.2. STORIES THE LIPS CAN TELL	
Lip Sign	**What It Means**
Lines or wrinkles	B_2 deficiency
Chapped	B_2 deficiency
Flakes of skin peel off	B_2 deficiency
Whistle marks on upper lip	B_2 deficiency
Upper lip gets smaller	B_2 deficiency
"Paper cuts" at corners of mouth	Lysine or B_2 deficiency
Sore lips	B_5, B_2, B_6, folic acid, or linoleic acid deficiency
Cold sores	Lysine, B_6, B_2, B_5, C deficiency, poor digestion
Hair over lips in women	Faulty pancreas function
Sore	Too much sugar or other acid-forming foods

Note: Never take individual B vitamins unless under the care of a nutritionist or nutritionally oriented doctor. Always take a complete B complex. It will contain at least eleven nutrients if it is complete.

CHANGE IS GOOD

I'm a firm believer that you can change things! There are many ways to do that. There is the easy way of taking a drug to cover up the symptom, or the other way of finding out what the problem means and doing something to correct it. It's up to you which you choose. You can be *re*active or *pro*active.

> A woman came to me for help. She had started to grow a mustache, and her husband wouldn't physically have anything to do with her anymore. So I gave her a questionnaire to fill out, and sure enough, she had symptoms showing that her pancreas was underfunctioning. She went on the suggested supplement, and in two weeks there was a noticeable reduction in her lip hair.

It Can Be Easier

Look at the diagram showing a hand being hit by a hammer (Figure 1.1 below). You can medicate yourself with any one of those remedies and the pain will go away. I know I've done nearly all of them over my lifetime. But wouldn't it be easier to just stop hitting your hand with the hammer? That's what the Anger Cure is all about. Stop hitting your hand! Well, you know what I mean: stop doing the things that are causing the imbalance that leads to the problem.

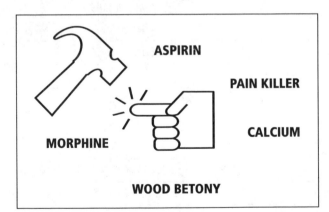

Figure 1.1

It's easy if you find that your lifelong struggle is really a B vitamin deficiency. You can just take B vitamins in pill form or eat a lot of foods that contain B vitamins. (See Appendix A for a list of foods rich in B vitamins.)

This book will discuss a variety of health problems—some people even go so far as to call them diseases—that you can reverse by just changing your lifestyle. It might not be easy, but with the proper diet and supplements many health problems will just melt away. I've seen it happen for thirty years! I know you will feel better, have less anger and temper tantrums, love more, enjoy life more, and be happier if you follow the Anger Cure.

"That can't be me, it doesn't sound like my symptoms, it doesn't even look like me. You must have the wrong chart." Hanna was returning for her six-week checkup after going on a nutritional program. She had none of the symptoms she had come in with six weeks earlier. The snapshot we took of her then didn't look the way she did now. She looked younger and felt great. So much so that she denied all her previous reasons for coming to the nutritional clinic in the first place. "I feel so good, I'm going to replace my forty-year-old husband with two twenty-year-olds," was her final comment.

LOOK AT YOUR HANDS

Now look at your hands. Is the skin rough, are there hangnails, yucky cuticles, or brown spots? Can you see all the veins easily because the skin is thin? Are your nails chipped, peeling, cracked? Is the nail bed raised up? Do you have warts? All these things are indications of nutritional deficiencies. Look at Table 1.3 on the following page and see which ones apply to your hands.

WHAT'S YOUR SCORE?

Look back at Tables 1.1–1.3. Did you have any of the signs of B vitamin deficiency? It really doesn't matter how many you had; one is enough. But chances are that you had more than one. Most people do. Look at the symptoms you checked off. Keep a record of these things with the date so you have some way of judging how well you're doing when you make the recommended simple changes.

WHAT THIS ALL MEANS

When you start to follow the complete Anger Cure, many of these vitamin deficiencies will just disappear. It's not a matter of taking an indi-

TABLE 1.3. STORIES THE HANDS CAN TELL	
HAND SIGN	WHAT IT MEANS
Cold	Poor circulation, B vitamin deficiency
Cracked and/or scaly	Vitamin B_6, B_5, essential fatty acids deficiency
Warts	Vitamins A and E deficiency
Swollen	Allergies, too much salt, stress, reduced calcium absorption
Trembling	Vitamin B_6 and magnesium, or B_5 deficiency
Brown or bronze spots	Stress, B_5 deficiency, adrenal overload, too much sun
Thin skin	Overactive thyroid, B vitamin deficiency
Dry skin	Liver bogged down, underactive thyroid
Nail weak, ridged	Stress, adrenal glands exhausted
Longitudinal ridges on nails	Anemia, iron and/or B vitamin deficiency
Thickened nail bed	Fungus infection
Hangnails	Vitamin C, protein, or folic acid deficiency
Split nails	Protein or vitamin A deficiency, poor digestion
Thin nails	Protein or vitamin A deficiency, poor digestion
White spots on nails	Vitamin B_6 and/or zinc deficiency

Note: Never take individual B vitamins unless under the care of a nutritionist or nutritionally oriented doctor. Always take a complete B complex. It will contain at least eleven nutrients if it is complete.

vidual nutrient, but rather of changing your lifestyle so that your body works at peek functioning all the time. Millions of people have made changes that have brought back a spring in their step, returned their natural hair color, reversed many of the tongue, lip, and hand symptoms, and really given them a new lease on life. If you want to feel better, fly off the handle less, love more, then the Anger Cure is for you. This is just the very beginning.

If you want to feel better, fly off the handle less, love more, then the Anger Cure is for you.

I met a man about sixty-five years old who had a huge brown spot suddenly show up on his face.

I blatantly said to him, "How long have you had diabetes?"

He shot me a shocked look and replied, "I don't."

"Would you like to get rid of that spot?" I asked.

"Love to," came his reply.

So I suggested he go to a health food store and purchase a good B complex vitamin and some extra B_5. (I gave him specific instructions on what to buy.)

Less than a month later, I saw him and the spot was gone! How's that for dealing with a deficiency? When you know what your body needs, it's easy to give it to yourself.

WHAT B COMPLEX VITAMINS DO

B complex vitamins are essential for health in so many different ways, it's impossible to include them all here. For example, B vitamins are necessary for the health of your skin, hair, eyes, liver, tongue and mouth, digestion, and even brain function. And they're necessary for energy, digestion of carbohydrates, preventing all kinds of intestinal problems, and they've been used to reduce depression, anxiety, alcoholism, and schizophrenia. Three that are getting the most press lately are B_6, B_{12}, and folic acid (which used to be called B_9). Many articles published in newspapers, weekly newsmagazines, and professional journals show they help reduce homocysteine, which is now thought to be the major cause of heart attacks and so many other kinds of aging symptoms. High levels of homocysteine are even reported to play a part in Alzheimer's disease.[1] Many older people have memory troubles that can be helped by taking B_{12}, either sublingual (dissolved under the tongue) or injected. Research published over the last seven or eight years has shown that low levels of folate or folic acid can lead to colon cancer.[2] The best source of folic acid is dark green leafy veggies. Parsley, romaine lettuce, watercress, kale, even spinach all contain folic acid.

I had an older friend who was having trouble with memory and energy. I suggested he eat liver once a week because I knew he wouldn't take vitamins. That did the trick for him. Liver is a good source of B vitamins, especially B_{12}. How long has it been since you ate liver?

B Vitamin Robbers

B vitamins are removed from wheat flour, rice, and sugar when they are refined. But people need B vitamins to help digest starch or carbohydrates. That means every time you eat refined white flour, white rice, or white sugar products you are robbing B vitamins from somewhere else in your body to help digest these denatured foods. That's why whole grains are needed for a healthy diet. Whole grains have not been refined so they contain the B complex vitamins necessary for proper digestion and utilization of the nutrients. If you are going to eat bread, rice, noodles, pasta of any kind, or sugar, please make sure it's unrefined and natural. Brown rice, whole wheat, pot barley, and unrefined sugar are the only way to eat these products if you want to remain healthy.

> *Every time you eat refined white flour, white rice, or white sugar products you are robbing B vitamins from somewhere else in your body to help digest these denatured foods.*

Eating white sugar and white flour products can actually cause fatigue, depression, anger attacks, anxiety, and reduced health. If you think drinking a sugar-laden soft drink all day is giving you energy, think again. It's robbing you of precious B complex vitamins! Even artificial sugars are bad for you because they can cause other health problems.

Alcohol is made from refined sugar. All kinds of alcoholic drinks rob you of the essential B complex vitamins you need to stay healthy. Many of the "beauty" problems of alcoholics are directly related to B vitamin deficiencies brought on by drinking alcohol and not eating dark green leafy vegetables, whole grains, and other sources of B complex vitamins.

Overcoming Stress Requires B Vitamins

B vitamins are necessary for eliminating stress. That's why so many B complex supplements are called something like "Stress Formula" and "Stress Tabs." If you have stress in your life—and who doesn't!—you'll need more B complex vitamins than usual. They will help you digest more efficiently, keep calm, sleep better, and be more alert. When you have the appropriate amount of B vitamins in your body, you won't have as much trouble with stress and anger. There's a lot more to overcoming stress and anger than just taking B complex vitamins, but it's a good start.

WHAT ARE THE B COMPLEX VITAMINS?

Most of the B vitamins go by numbers, but there are coenzymes and other forms that do not. Vitamins B_1, B_2, B_3, B_5, B_6, and B_{12} are all called by numbers, and biotin, choline, folate or folic acid, PABA, and inositol are called by names. If you take a B complex supplement, all eleven of these ingredients should be in it. (See Appendix A for the actual names of the individual vitamins.)

How Much, How Many?

B complex vitamins are heat-, light-, and water-soluble. That means they have to be replenished several times a day. It is important to take them three times a day in a low dose rather than once a day in a high dose. I consider 12 to 25 milligrams (mg) of each of the B vitamins enough for most people to take in each low-dose supplement. Fifty to 100 mg is considered a high dose and is not necessary except under severe stress. A sustained or timed-release B complex vitamin of 50 mg is fine because it will be released into your system over four to six hours, but you will need to take one with your morning meal and one with your evening meal for it to be most effective.

Always Take Vitamins and Minerals with Food!

Chewing starts digestion, and supplements need digestive enzymes to break them down and be absorbed.

Pill or powder forms of vitamins and minerals are called food supplements: they supplement your food and should always be taken with food. Chewing starts digestion, and supplements need digestive enzymes to break them down and be absorbed. Taking supplements with food helps your body use them best and get the most from them. Whatever amount of B vitamins your body doesn't need at a given time is excreted. If you take them alone, you might be excreting all the nutrients in the supplements. What a waste of money and good vitamins!

WHAT'S THE VERDICT?

Did you see any B complex vitamin-deficiency signs on your tongue, lips, or hands? If so, the Anger Cure can help you. Start today to change your lifestyle and begin eating B-vitamin-rich whole foods. Read the label of everything you eat. Does it have sugar? White flour? White rice? Exchange it for whole and more natural foods.

CHAPTER SUMMARY

1. Many vitamin and mineral deficiencies are indicated by the spots, lines, wrinkles, and other telltale marks on your tongue, lips, and hands. They can easily be corrected with diet and lifestyle changes.

2. A lot of problems classified as diseases can be avoided by monitoring your nutritional deficiencies and making recommended changes. The sooner you recognize a symptom and do something about it, the better chance you have of avoiding serious health problems later.

3. All B complex vitamins are important for your total health.

CHAPTER 2

The Hidden Killer of Relationships and Love

My friend Danny was in the hospital for panic attacks and anxiety. While I was visiting him, they brought him some coffee. I immediately went to his doctor and reported the nurses who had done this. The doctor was livid that they were giving him coffee. He stopped the coffee and my friend recovered quickly. Danny didn't realize that the caffeinated colas he drank by the quart every day had caused his panic and anxiety problem in the first place. How could the nurses not know this? I guess they have to do whatever the patient wants as long as it keeps them quiet and isn't against the doctor's orders.

Anger, panic, fear, anxiety, depression, and fatigue are just a few of the many symptoms of low blood sugar, or hypoglycemia as it is often called by holistic practitioners. If you want to see if this is an issue in your health, take the Low Blood Sugar Test. If you pass, go on to the next chapter. If you score high, then this chapter is for you.

TAKE THE LOW BLOOD SUGAR TEST

Take the test on the following page yourself, and then have a family member or close friend take it for you. Compare the answers and assume that you are somewhere in between your answers and your family member's or friend's answers.

LOW BLOOD SUGAR TEST

Put 0, 1, 2, or 3, on the line next to all the symptoms that in any way apply to you, no matter how mild they seem to be. The value to you of this survey depends on your honest, objective answers. Take your time!

- Use "0" if you have never had it.
- Use "1" if it is mild—you have it once or twice a year.
- Use "2" if it is moderate—you have it monthly or several times a year.
- Use "3" if it is severe—you have it daily or weekly or you may not always have the symptoms, but you are always aware that you have the problem.

_1_ Allergies	_1_ Drowsiness	_1_ Leg cramps
_3_ Anger/rage	_2_ Excessive hunger	_3_ Muscle aches/pains
_3_ Anxiety	_3_ Exhaustion	_2_ Muscular twitching
_1_ Blurred vision	_3_ Faintness	_3_ Nervousness
_1_ Cold sweats	_2_ Fears	_3_ Nightmares
_2_ Compulsive eating	_3_ Forgetfulness	_3_ Personality changes
_1_ Confusion	_2_ Headaches	___ Poor coordination
_0_ Convulsions	___ Indecisiveness	___ Sighing/yawning
_3_ Crave sugar/starches	_3_ Insomnia	___ Skip breakfast
_2_ Crying spells	_3_ Irregular meals	___ Staggering
_3_ Depression	_3_ Irritability	___ Weak spells
_2_ Dizziness/tremors	_3_ Lack of sex drive	___ **TOTAL SCORE**

What's Your Score?

Add the numbers together—2 + 3 + 1 = 6 and so forth—until you have the total number. What was your total? 105? 75? 53? 25? 15? This may surprise you, but if you scored higher than 15 on this test, chances are really great that you have fluctuating blood sugar problems that contribute to your anger and rage. (You'll learn more about this in Chapter 7.)

Bigger Isn't Always Better

If you got a score around 15, that doesn't mean that you are ill or have a disease. It might not even mean that these things debilitate you. It does mean that you are out of balance, and you should consider low blood sugar part of your health problem. If you have anger or rage, then this questionnaire should be an eye opener for you. There is a connection between your blood sugar levels and your anger levels.

If you have anger or rage, then this questionnaire should be an eye opener for you.

Jon got a score of 25 on the Low Blood Sugar Test. Every night he came home from work, went into his bedroom, and cried for an hour or so. He said he couldn't help himself; he had to do it. He wasn't sure if he was depressed; he just felt like crying. That was the main reason we suspected he had a blood sugar fluctuation problem.

WATCH OUT FOR BIGI

The late Vickers Head was a pioneer in the area of blood sugar problems and led a group that gave lectures on and provided support for what he called BIGI, or blood insulin glucose imbalance. His CHADA (Canadian Hypoglycemia and Dietetic Awareness) society gave seminars on hypoglycemia and hypothyroidism and other related topics in the 1970s and 1980s in Toronto, Ontario. He was a tireless advocate for all who needed his help. I learned a lot from him. He was one of the first people to talk about the insulin balance problem. However, medical doctors are still not talking about the insulin balance problem even though solving it unlocks the door to good health. Diet and special herbs are the keys. The Anger Cure is the outcome of that research. Head called BIGI "the Hidden Killer of Personality, Relationships, and People." I have seen many relationships killed by this problem.

Personality, Relationships, People

If you have constant anxiety and fear of insanity, if you feel worthless or helpless, if you have depression or a wide variation in your moods and energy, if you snap at people or are angry, then you fall under Head's category of Hidden Killer of Personality. If you have problems in relationships due to a difficult personality, an inability to communicate effectively, insensitivity toward other people, or sexual or other incompatibilities, you fall under his category of Killer of Relationships. If you sometimes have accidents due to a lack of concentration, poor reactions, and/or impatience or even feel suicidal, then you fall under his category of Killer of People.

> John was having a meeting in his country kitchen with other workers from the gym. His wife was outside working in the garden. Suddenly, she burst through the door yelling at him. As he stood up, she came at him and started pounding on his chest while continuing to yell. It wasn't even clear to John why she was angry at him. She left in a fit of rage. One of the fitness instructors asked if John's wife had eaten breakfast, since it was now 11 A.M. Yeah, she had the same breakfast she had every day: a can or two of cola. John's wife was living in a constantly induced angry state. She often got angry with her students at school and flew off the handle at them, too.

Love

Most low blood sugar symptoms are anti-love. Hypoglycemia in and of itself can stop you from loving. Who can love when they are depressed, angry, or anxious? Total health means being able to love and love unconditionally. Can you do that? It's nearly impossible when you have BIGI or hypoglycemia. You are also unlovable. You might have allergies, be in pain, or be cranky, and that can make you seem unlovable. You might not even love yourself because of these things. How can you expect someone else to love you? Hypoglycemia problems can also be the cause of many kinds of low self-esteem, lack of initiative, and what might be called laziness. My mother used to describe her low blood sugar times like this: "My get-up-and-go got up and went."

BASIC UNIT OF ENERGY

The basic unit of energy or fuel in your body comes from blood sugar, and blood sugar comes from food and drink. If you put fuel in your body, it will work; if you try to run it without fuel, it will break down.

FOOD = ENERGY
NO FOOD = NO ENERGY

Since blood sugar is the basic unit of energy for every part of your body, it stands to reason that eating food will give you energy. Therefore food = energy. The opposite is also true. No food = no energy. This is a simple principle that you might have learned in school: You need to eat to have energy.

Every part of your body runs on this very basic fuel. Your brain, muscles, organs, everything! If you try to make your brain work without this basic fuel, it will cause problems. If you do physical activity without eating first, you could cause a muscle spasm in your heart from which you might never recover. After all, without fuel, your heart can't function optimally. I often wonder how many seniors who have heart attacks shoveling snow in the winter ate breakfast before they tried to make their heart work so hard. I suspect that many of them didn't eat or had something that didn't serve as fuel for their heart muscle. When they called upon their heart to work, there was no fuel, so it couldn't function.

LOW BLOOD SUGAR

When you don't eat and your body doesn't get the blood sugar it needs to function, that condition is called low blood sugar. As you might suspect, there is a lot more to it than just this simple explanation, and we will get into that gradually.

In holistic medical terms low blood sugar is often called hypoglycemia, which means the same thing: "hypo" means low and "glycemia" means blood sugar. Many doctors were taught in medical school that hypoglycemia can only happen when there are two circumstances: an insulin-secreting tumor and an insulin reaction from injections. So if your doctor tells you this discussion of low blood sugar is bunk, just remember that we are on the cutting edge of this, not your doctor, who may not be keeping up with the latest information on nutrition.

Drug companies are now pushing several drugs that they say will help low blood sugar. They call the condition "type 2 diabetes" because they produce a drug that addresses this problem. However, they are not looking at the entire picture. Someone may have an insulin-sensitivity problem that they don't recognize as full-blown diabetes. We will discuss this in more detail in Chapter 5.

Depression

The American Diabetes Association notes that diabetes (a blood sugar problem discussed in greater detail below) doubles the risk for depression, including the symptoms of irritability, social withdrawal, and indecisiveness. All these symptoms are in the Low Blood Sugar Test. Research done in Korea by Yonsei University showed that people with depression are more likely to have anger or hostility problems than people who just have anxiety or people who are otherwise healthy. The study also found that the more depressed a person was the more anger they expressed.[1]

As you may have noticed, some of the signs and symptoms of depression (see sidebar) are also symptoms of low blood sugar. If you have depression, please do not stop taking any medication prescribed for you by your doctor. Read this book through and then tell your doctor you are going on a special program. Get your doctor's approval before you make any changes, and do not stop any medication without approval. It may take days, weeks, or even months for you to feel better on the Anger Cure program, so don't make any changes in medication until your doctor tells you it's suitable to do so.

Signs and Symptoms of Depression

- Sadness
- Loss of energy
- Feelings of hopelessness or worthlessness
- Loss of enjoyment
- Difficulty concentrating
- Uncontrollable crying
- Difficulty making decisions
- Irritability
- Increased need for sleep
- Unexplained aches and pains
- Insomnia or excessive sleeping
- Decreased sex drive
- Sexual problems
- Headache
- Change in appetite causing weight gain or loss
- Thoughts of death or suicide
- Attempting suicide

Menopause

"Can you help me with a problem my wife has? I think it's her age or change of life or something," a client's husband asked. He called it "bites husband's head off for no reason." My client had never mentioned this to me, but her husband sure did!

Many women experience mood swings, fatigue, anger, rage, memory loss, and low sex drive during the years leading up to menopause. This time is often called perimenopause or premenopause. Keeping your blood sugar balanced with the Anger Cure diet and supplement suggestions will help. You might also need to use some herbal female hormonal support or progesterone cream. Many women's supplements are available in health food stores. The basic ingredients that help with menopause symptoms are black cohosh, dong quai, chaste berry, and wild yam. Progesterone cream, which is rubbed on various parts of the body daily, should contain between 25 and 30 mg of natural progesterone derived from wild yam. I've seen many women overcome fatigue and memory loss in just a few days by using progesterone cream and following a blood-sugar-balancing diet like the Anger Cure.

Low Sex Drive

Generally, when a person scores more than 15 on the Low Blood Sugar Test, he or she has low sex drive and/or low sexual response. A yeast problem might also be at fault. For more information on the yeast connection to low blood sugar and low sex drive, see Chapter 6.

You will have less reason to use a prescription for erectile dysfunction if you stabilize your blood sugar and eat the correct foods at the correct times.

If you marked lack of sex drive on the Low Blood Sugar Test, then the Anger Cure program and supplements will really help you. You will have less reason to use a prescription for erectile dysfunction if you stabilize your blood sugar and eat the correct foods at the correct times.

Mrs. Scott, a sweet little birdlike lady of seventy–five years old, came up to me at the clinic with the Low Blood Sugar Test in her hand and said, "How do I know if I have low sex drive? My husband's been gone for ten years." How times have changed! What adult who lived through the sexual revolution of the 1960s and 1970s even thinks of needing a partner to have sex drive?

The Diabetes Epidemic

According to the American Diabetes Association, 17 million people in the United States have diabetes, but as many as 5.9 million sufferers are unaware they have the disease. Diabetes is the name generally given to a blood sugar problem. Three kinds are now recognized: type 1, type 2, and prediabetes. Prediabetes is what has been called hypoglycemia by holistic practitioners, nutritionists, and natural practicing physicians for thirty years. In the 1990s, because more and more people were having trouble with blood sugar fluctuations because of high-carbohydrate diets and the standard American diet, drugs were invented to help with blood sugar problems. Consequently more people are now being diagnosed as having type 2 diabetes or prediabetes. This has reached epidemic pro-portions. However, it is generally recognized that by eating correctly and keeping your weight down you can beat type 2 and prediabetes.

STUDY YOUR SCORE

Look at your score on the Low Blood Sugar Test. Look closely at the symptoms that you scored a 2 or 3. Are these your main health problems? Did you know you had these problems? If you follow the Anger Cure pro-gram of lifestyle changes and supplements, most of the problems you marked off will no longer be a problem. I wish I could tell you how long it will take to completely get over them, but I can't. It depends on you: how well you follow the program, how long you have had this imbalance, and a host of other factors we'll talk about later.

All or Nowhere

I can assure you that you will gain your health and reverse anger and rage if you follow the Anger Cure completely. That's the "all" part. If you do not, you may end up "nowhere." Make a a pact with yourself to follow the Anger Cure program for two weeks. Sign the following form.

I _____ agree to follow the Anger Cure program faithfully for two weeks beginning _____ .

If, after two weeks, I see any improvement in my health, anger level, rage level, or any of the symptoms I marked a 2 or 3 on the Low Blood Sugar Test, I will continue for another two weeks.

Signed: _____ *Dated:* _____

By making this agreement with yourself and signing it, you will start taking charge of your health and life.

HOW TO BEGIN

There are a lot of things you can do to begin the Anger Cure. You can eliminate foods from your lifestyle that trigger blood sugar drops like coffee, tea, cigarettes, sugar and anything sweet (even a nonsugar sweetener), white flour, white rice, and all processed and chemical-laden foodstuffs. When you go shopping, just shop in the outside aisles in the produce, dairy, meat, poultry, and fish sections. Don't buy cookies, candy, white flour pasta, white breads and other bakery products, or processed meats like bologna, salami, bacon, or processed cheeses. Avoid prepared and packaged foods as they generally contain MSG, sodium, sugar, maltodextrose, and artificial colors and/or flavors.

Small, Frequent Meals

Eating small, frequent meals (SFM) is the second thing you can do to start the Anger Cure. Eat five or six small meals spaced out during the day, starting with breakfast when you first get up. Or eat three small meals and three small snacks. Either way you do it, you will feel better and have more energy. You will also find that you are not as likely to have anger come up when you eat this way.

Breakfast Is King

"The general rule, however, is to eat breakfast like a king, lunch like a prince, and dinner like a pauper," wrote Adelle Davis, the mother of modern nutrition.[2]

Why is the first meal of the day called breakfast? Because it literally means to "break the fast." You have gone six to ten hours without eating—a mini-fast in effect. That means your blood sugar is low when you get up. In order for your brain to work you need to eat something to give you the blood sugar energy to think. When your blood sugar drops, you can't tell if you're hungry. So it's no wonder many people don't eat breakfast: They can't think enough to do it.

Breakfast gives you the energy your body needs to work.

FOOD = ENERGY
NO FOOD = NO ENERGY

It's important to eat breakfast within a half hour of getting up. That can make or break your day. Your body needs good food first thing in the morning if you want to avoid anger, memory problems, lack of coordination, allergies, poor digestion, and all the other things in the Low Blood Sugar Test.

Did you know that just one day of not eating breakfast can throw you off for several days? You may not want to eat breakfast, but you will have to make yourself to regain a healthy balance. Just check yourself out. Do you find you have more stress when you don't eat breakfast? Do you forget things, bump into things, drop things, have the sniffles, yell at people, sleep more, lose your temper, or have anger on days when you don't eat breakfast?

Look at the Low Blood Sugar Test. All the items you marked are the things that happen to your body when you don't eat right. And eating breakfast is part of eating right. You can end the cycle of low blood sugar problems by eating small, frequent meals starting with breakfast first thing in the morning and eliminating all the items from your lifestyle that trigger sudden or extreme blood sugar changes.

Breakfast should be the biggest meal of the day. Of course, you want to stay away from white flour, refined cereals, sugar products like jam and sweet rolls, and coffee. If you choose to eat a whole-grain cereal, look at the label. If sugar, sucrose, dextrose, maltose, or high fructose corn sweeteners are in it, don't eat it. I suggest a small amount of protein and vegetables or vegetable juice for breakfast. A natural cheese sandwich on whole-grain bread with lettuce or other veggies is a good start to the day. I like to have a lamb chop and raw veggies for breakfast. When I was in high school, I had my mother make ground beef into little patties. Most mornings I would cook one and eat whatever veggies were left over from dinner. Those were the days I felt best, had lots of energy, and could think.

An old-fashioned farm breakfast consisted of fried chicken, pork chops, bacon, eggs, veggies, potatoes, gravy, biscuits, and whole-grain breads. These are the kinds of foods that provide the energy needed to do heavy work on a farm. You don't need to eat all that if you're not doing heavy work. If you drive a truck, sit at a desk, work in a store, take care of children, or any number of jobs that require energy, but are not heavy physical work, you will need to eat a good breakfast but not a heavy one.

"Breakfast Doesn't Work for Me"

Many people have told me over the years that they can't eat breakfast. My response is: "Then you ate too much or ate too late the night before, or you skipped breakfast or lunch." Others say that if they eat breakfast, they are hungry in a few hours so they just don't eat breakfast. My response is, "Then you ate something with sugar or white flour products for breakfast and it made you get hungry too fast."

"I Don't Have Time for Breakfast"

Since every part of your body, including your brain, needs blood sugar to function, if you have no blood sugar in your body, you can't think or get organized. Simply taking some vegetable juice, either plain or with unsweetened protein powder, first thing in the morning could provide enough nutrition to your brain so you can think better and organize your time better to be able to eat breakfast. If you want coffee or a cigarette to get you going, you need to eat something like vegetable juice first thing to bring up your blood sugar levels. Do not rely on the false energy of cigarettes or coffee.

Why Are Coffee and Cigarettes Bad for You?

Food = Energy
Cigarettes = Fatigue, Anger, Rage, Exhaustion, and Aging

Coffee and cigarettes trigger the fight-or-flight response that raises your blood sugar so you can think. (See Chapter 8 for details about the fight-or-flight response.) However, it's a false high that only lasts a few hours or less. Then your blood sugar levels drop and you want more cigarettes and coffee. By the end of the day you will not have eaten and you will be tired. You will also think you're addicted to cigarettes. And you are! You're addicted to using tobacco to substitute for food and to raise your blood sugar levels. This is the quickest way to age fast, develop anger and rage, and trigger all kinds of health problems. Try eating food instead of having a cigarette. You might be surprised that after a few weeks, or perhaps even days, you don't want cigarettes anymore. Remember that food = energy. And cigarettes = fatigue, anger, rage, exhaustion, and aging.

> Jim was on disability because of panic disorder. He lived on cigarettes and heavily sugared coffee. Several of us told him the coffee and cigarettes might be responsible for his health problems. He was so angry he flew into a rage, went wild, and had to be held back. He agreed later to give up cigarettes and coffee and to start eating breakfast. Wow, what a difference, no more panic attacks, no more violent outbursts.

Is There a Pill?

Sometimes it's very difficult to get out of the cycle of not eating or eating incorrectly without some additional help. That's why your health food store has a lot of supplements for stabilizing your blood sugar. Most of the formulas contain a combination of nutrients like GTF chromium, vanadyl sulfate, momordica extract (bitter melon), gymnema sylvestre, fenugreek seed, and alpha-lipoic acid. This combination of minerals and herbs has been shown to effectively stabilize blood sugar levels.

Many people who have fluctuating blood sugar levels are actually low in the mineral chromium. Chromium is removed from grains that are processed, and current farming methods don't recognize the importance of having chromium in the soil. Chromium is also necessary if you eat a lot of dairy products, grains, or other carbohydrates.

Gymnema sylvestre and bitter melon are two herbs that have been used for many years in India to help keep blood sugar levels from going too high or dropping too low. If you would like more information on this, go to www.angercure.com.

Even if you decide to get help faster by taking a supplement that keeps your blood sugar levels stabilized, you must still eat breakfast and small, frequent meals and stay away from coffee, cigarettes, sugar, and other carbohydrates. It's not necessary to follow a low fat diet. In fact, it's been shown that the low-fat, high-carbohydrate diet is often responsible for causing the blood sugar fluctuation problem in the first place.[3]

> "I started on the Anger Cure supplements after taking the test, and I have had several interesting responses," Ricky told me. "For one, I don't have the taste or need for beer. The second good thing was that I don't have headaches anymore. And I can't remember a time when I didn't have them. The Anger Cure lifestyle plan and supplements are fantastic! P.S. I also don't have angry flare-ups at my family and coworkers anymore either."

NIP IT IN THE BUD

As soon as you feel something triggering a panic or anger reaction, stop and breathe deeply. (See Chapter 3 for breathing instructions.) Take charge of your body. In other words, don't let your body run you. While you are doing slow, deep breathing, check out your diet for the day. Did you have coffee, sugar, tobacco, or go without eating? These are all things that can bring on anger, panic, and shallow breathing leading to lack of confidence and panic. Could you have an undisclosed allergy that triggered the drop in your blood sugar and brought on feelings of panic leading to the fight-or-flight response? If you suspect that something you ate or touched caused this, have yourself tested for allergies by a reputable holistic allergist or environmental medicine specialist, who will also work with you on your diet and lifestyle. Environmental medicine is all about the substances we come in contact with that cause reactions.

The first foods to look at are dairy products, chicken and eggs, oranges, corn, wheat, potatoes, and anything with chemicals or additives like MSG and other excitotoxins. If you feel bad after a Chinese meal, you can generally assume it contained MSG. However, fermented foods could cause a reaction, too (see Chapter 6).

Easy Allergy Test

If you have sensitivities to foods, it's easy to test for them. Just don't eat any foods with the ingredient you suspect you are sensitive to for at least three or four full days. Then eat the food once. If you have a reaction, it is most likely a problem for you. Just remember that blood sugar and yeast problems often weaken your body and make you seem allergic or sensitive to foods when you are not. If you have a true allergy that you have been tested for, please do not do the rotation diet challenge below without your doctor's approval.

Eating so you avoid allergies is actually called a rotation diet because you rotate food groups every four days (since it generally takes three days for your body to recover). If you eat foods more frequently than that, you could be undermining your body's defenses. Then your body will break down and produce symptoms of an allergy.

You should know that for the most part I use allergy and addiction interchangeably in this book. I really mean food sensitivity, not true allergy. Any food that makes you feel really good—you're addicted to. It could be sugar, white flour, corn, alcohol, fruit, chewing gum, dairy products, or any number of other foods. When you eat the same foods day after day, you can develop a sensi-

> *Any food that makes you feel really good—you're addicted to. It could be sugar, white flour, corn, alcohol, fruit, chewing gum, dairy products, or any number of other foods.*

tivity to them that undermines your health. Then it becomes difficult to get off them because you are addicted to the things the foods do to you. Once you try to stop, the withdrawal symptoms seem worse than the symptoms you get from eating them.

> I was visiting a relative once who told me that he just had to have corn chips. He even kept them in the glove compartment of his car so he didn't have to stop to buy them while he was traveling. He also drank a lot of soft drinks sweetened with high-fructose corn syrup. It turned out he was so allergic to corn that he'd become addicted to it. I noticed that he had such a problem with diarrhea, it bordered on irritable bowel problems. He must have really been in pain when he didn't get the corn and had to go through withdrawal.

Rotation Diet Challenge

To do the rotation diet challenge, divide all the foods you eat into food groups. Broccoli, cabbage, collard greens, and Brussels sprouts are in the same family, so only eat them one day of the week and stay away from them for the next three days. Then you can eat them on the fourth day. Nightshade foods like green peppers, eggplant, tomatoes, and potatoes can be another day. Just look at the foods you eat daily as the starting point. Only test for one food group at a time. The biological classification of foods listings will help you separate the foods you eat into food groups.

To challenge yourself for dairy products, don't eat anything with milk, cream, cheese, cottage cheese, cream cheese, butter, milk solids, whey, casein, or any other dairy products in it. Look at the labels on the foods you eat. You might be surprised what foods have milk or milk solids in them.

Look at the labels on the foods you eat.

Keep a Log

The best way to track a problem is to keep a log of what you do every day. Write down what you eat, what you touch, what you breathe in, and any reactions. If every time you touch rubber, you get a rash, you'll know that you are sensitive to rubber. If every time you eat eggs, your hands swell, you'll know that eggs are the cause. Constant vigilance will show you what is affecting you.

Biological Classification of Foods

GRAINS
Barley
  malt
  flour
  pearl
  pot
Cane
  sugar
  molasses
Corn
  cornstarch
  corn oil
  corn syrup
  cellulose
  dextrose
  glucose
Oat
  bran
  groats
  rolled
  oatmeal
Rice
  brown
  white
  basmati
  refined
  polished
Rye
Sorghum
Wheat
  flour
  gluten
  bran
  wheat germ
Wild rice

SPURGE FAMILY
Tapioca

ARROWROOT FAMILY
Arrowroot

ARUM FAMILY
Taro
  poi

BUCKWHEAT FAMILY
Buckwheat
Rhubarb

NIGHTSHADE OR POTATO FAMILY
Chili
Eggplant
Green pepper
Potato
Red pepper
  cayenne
Tomato

COMPOSITE FAMILY
Artichoke
Chicory
Dandelion
Endive
Escarole
Head lettuce
Leaf lettuce
Oyster plant
(salsify)

LEGUMES
Acacia
Black-eyed peas
Kidney beans
Lentils
Licorice
Lima beans
Navy beans
Pea
Peanut
  peanut oil
  peanut butter

Senna
Soybeans
  soybean oil
  tofu
  tempeh
  lecithin
String beans

MUSTARD FAMILY
Broccoli
Brussels sprouts
Cabbage
Cauliflower
Celery cabbage
  napa
Collard
Horseradish
Kale
Kohlrabi
Mustard
  greens
  seeds
Radish
Rutabaga
Turnip
Watercress

GOURD FAMILY
Cantaloupe
Casaba
Cucumber
Honeydew
Muskmelon
Persian melon
Pumpkin
Squash
Watermelon

LILY FAMILY
Aloes
Asparagus
Chive

Garlic
Leek
Onion
Shallot

GOOSEFOOT FAMILY
Beet
  root
  sugar
  greens
Spinach
Swiss chard

PARSLEY FAMILY
Anise
Caraway
Carrot
Celeriac
Celery
Coriander
Dill
Fennel
Parsley
Parsnip

MORNING GLORY FAMILY
Sweet Potato
Yam

SUNFLOWER FAMILY
Jerusalem artichoke
Sunflower seeds
  oil

POMEGRANATE FAMILY
Grenadine syrup
Pomegranate

EBONY FAMILY
Persimmon

ROSE FAMILY
Blackberry
Dewberry
Loganberry
Marionberry
Raspberry
Rose petals
Rose water
Strawberry
Youngberry

BANANA FAMILY
Banana

APPLE FAMILY
Apple
  cider
  cider vinegar
  pectin
  jam and jelly
  thickeners
Pear
Quince
  seeds
  jelly

PLUM FAMILY
Almond
Apricot
Cherry
Nectarine
Peach
Plum
  prune

LAUREL FAMILY
Avocado
  oil
Bay leaves
Cinnamon

OLIVE FAMILY
Green olive
Ripe olive
  olive oil
  olive leaf extract

HEATH FAMILY
Blueberry
Cranberry

GOOSEBERRY FAMILY
Current
  jelly
  dried
  juice
Gooseberry

HONEYSUCKLE FAMILY
Elderberry
  juice
  tea

PINEAPPLE FAMILY
Pineapple
  juice

PAPAYA FAMILY
Papaya
  juice
  dried

CITRUS FAMILY
Grapefruit
  juice
Kumquat
Lemon
  juice
Lime
  juice
Mercot
Orange
  juice
Tangerine
  juice

GRAPE FAMILY
Cream of tartar
Grape
  juice

filler in other
juices
Raisin

MYRTLE FAMILY
Allspice
Cloves
Guava
Paprika
Pimento

MINT FAMILY
Marjoram
Mint
Peppermint
Sage
Savory
Spearmint
Thyme

PEPPER FAMILY
Black pepper
  ground
  corns
White pepper

NUTMEG FAMILY
Nutmeg

GINGER FAMILY
Cardamom
Ginger
  root
  ground
Turmeric

PINE FAMILY
Juniper
Pycnogenol

ORCHID FAMILY
Vanilla

MADDER FAMILY
Coffee

TEA FAMILY
Tea

PEDALIUM FAMILY
Sesame seeds
  oil

MALLOW FAMILY
Cottonseed oil
Okra
  gumbo

STERCULA FAMILY
Chocolate
Cocoa

BIRCH FAMILY
Filbert
Hazelnut
Oil of birch
  wintergreen

MULBERRY FAMILY
Breadfruit
Fig
Hops
  beer
  ale
Mulberry

MAPLE FAMILY
Maple sugar
Maple syrup

PALM FAMILY
Coconut
Date
  sugar
Sage

LECYTHIS FAMILY
Brazil nut

POPPY FAMILY
Poppy seed

WALNUT FAMILY
Black walnut
Butternut
English walnut

Hickory nut
Pecan

CASHEW FAMILY
Cashew
Mango
Pistachio

BEECH FAMILY
Chestnut
Fungi
Mushrooms
Yeast

MISCELLANEOUS
Honey

MOLLUSKS
Abalone
Clam
Mussel
Oyster
Scallop
Squid

CRUSTACEANS
Crab
Crayfish
Lobster
Shrimp

REPTILES
Rattlesnake
Turtle

BIRDS
Chicken
  eggs
Duck
  eggs
Goose
  eggs
Grouse
Guinea hen
Partridge
Pheasant
Squab
Turkey

MAMMALS
Bear
Beef
  veal
  milk
  butter
  cheese
  gelatin
Buffalo
Elk
Goat
  milk
  cheese
Horse
Moose
Mutton
  lamb

Pork
  ham
  bacon
Raccoon
Reindeer
Squirrel
Venison
Whale

FISH
Anchovy
Barracuda
Black bass
Bluefish
Buffalo fish
Bullhead
Butterfish
Carp
Catfish
Chub
Cod
Croaker
Cusk
Drum
Eel
Flounder
Haddock
Hake
Harvest fish
Herring
Ling cod

Mackerel
Mullet
Muskellunge
Perch
Pickerel
Pike
Pollack
Pompano
Porgy
Rosefish
Salmon
Sardine
Scrod
Scup
Sea bass
Shad
Smelt
Snapper
Sole
Sturgeon
  caviar
Sucker
Sunfish
Swordfish
Tilapia
Trout
Tuna
Turbot
Weakfish
Whitefish

"My hands are swollen," Betty said to me one day.

"Did you eat eggs this morning?" I asked.

"Yes," she snapped, "what has that got to do with it?"

"I think you are allergic to or sensitive to eggs," I replied.

"Geeze, you are a nutcase," she flipped back at me.

Days later she approached me with a sheepish grin and said, "I think you're right. Every time I eat eggs for breakfast I have swollen fingers. I've got an appointment with an allergist to have it checked out."

Test for Allergic-like Sensitivities

When you have an allergic-like reaction, there is swelling in the tissues some place in the body. This, in turn, traps acid in the cells, causing aches and pains, anxiety, or needing a cigarette. Often the feeling of "coming down with something" is really an allergic reaction, not the flu or a cold.

One way to tell if you're having a sensitivity reaction is to take something that is very alkaline in order to reverse the acid held in the cells. Try drinking a teaspoon of baking soda in a small glass of water. If it tastes too bad, add some lemon juice. Did your symptoms subside?

The baking soda reverses the chemicals at the cellular level, which reverses the reaction. You then can pinpoint the allergy, take a homeopathic remedy for that specific thing, use the rotation diet, have an allergist test you and make an antidote, or stop eating or doing whatever is causing your sensitivity.

The Cause and the Cure

"I eat health food and exercise every day, and yet I can't give up smoking," my nutrition–counseling client said to me. "My family won't eat any healthy food until I give up cigarettes, I'm just beside myself about it. I need them."

"When do you want a cigarette the most?" I asked.

His reply was a little shocking, "Right after I eat lunch."

"And what do you have for lunch?"

"I have a sandwich on my homemade whole–wheat bread. I grind the flour myself every other day to make the bread."

"Do you eat it every day?"

"Yes," he replied.

"Well, that's it. You have developed a sensitivity to wheat by eating it every day. Give up the wheat for several days and see what happens."

He did and lost the desire for cigarettes.

Cigarettes and baking soda are the two most alkaline substances that can reverse the acid trapped in your cells from an allergy/sensitivity. What we came to realize was that the man in the case study ate the wheat, had the swelling, and smoked cigarettes. Every time his blood sugar dropped from the allergy, he used cigarettes to raise his blood sugar and relieve his reaction. Then he became sensitive to the cigarettes themselves and smoked more to relieve the swelling from the cigarette allergy and the drops in his blood sugar. He was trapped. So he followed my suggestions. First, he took the baking soda drink when he wanted a cigarette to prove to himself that this was the case. It worked. Then he gave up eating wheat every day and followed a rotation diet with the wheat, and he no longer needed the cigarettes.

There Is a Better Way

A better way to solve an allergy/sensitivity problem is to figure out why your body is so sensitive in the first place. Many things can weaken your body and we will deal with each of them in turn. Often I have seen people with multiple allergies eliminate all of them once they have stabilized their blood sugar levels.

A professional man came to the clinic where I worked. He was on a so-called bland diet. He could only eat white rice, mashed potatoes, and milk products. He was supposedly allergic to about twenty-five foods. He was so hyper, so angry, and so negative that the receptionist would go out in the hall while he was in the waiting room. She couldn't even be in the same room with him!

After we did a work-up on him and stabilized his blood sugar levels, it turned out he was not allergic to any of the things on his list. The bland diet was not giving him enough nourishment to be healthy, and it was throwing off his blood sugar so he seemed to be more and more allergic. Once he started following the recommendations, he became calm, pleasant, and not at all allergic. The receptionist even started to like him and looked forward to his visits. His anger and rage was the direct result of his diet and lifestyle.

CHAPTER SUMMARY

1. Taking the Low Blood Sugar Test shows you aspects of your life that are affected by fluctuating blood sugar levels due to your lifestyle.

2. Food = energy, and no food = no energy.

3. Small, frequent meals are the solution to blood sugar problems along with avoiding substances that lower your blood sugar levels.

4. You may need to change your lifestyle to eliminate white flour and sugar products, caffeine, nicotine, processed and chemical-laden foods, alcohol, and gum.

5. Food sensitivities can affect your blood sugar.

6. Use the rotation diet to address blood sugar problems brought on by sensitivities.

CHAPTER 3

Lips Together/ Teeth Apart

"OK, everybody, lips together/teeth apart. Bring the sound up to the front of your face; you should feel it buzzing behind your lips on your front teeth as you bring the sound into your nasal cavity. We call this humming!"
Mr. Kochenderfer began directing the choir to hum our new piece
for the Southfield High School spring concert.

Lips together/teeth apart is the basic instruction for humming. It is also the basic instruction for stress and/or anger management. Look at your jaw in the mirror. Catch yourself in a store window. Is your jaw moving? Look at everybody you meet for the next week. Look especially in the line at the bank and the grocery store where people are standing close

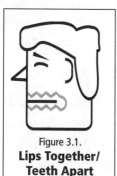

Figure 3.1.
Lips Together/ Teeth Apart

to you and are under stress. Are their jaws moving? Is there a little muscle in their jaw that moves or pulsates? Are they grinding or clenching their teeth because of stress? If they had their lips together/teeth apart they wouldn't be moving their jaw muscles!

TAKE THE JAW TENSION TEST

Now take the test on page 44 to see if you have tension in your jaw.

LIPS TOGETHER/TEETH APART EXERCISES

Try the following exercises to help relieve tension and relax your jaw.

JAW TENSION TEST

Look in a well-lit mirror. Mark off all that apply, and give yourself 1 point for each mark.

_____ Mouth looks like a frown.

_____ Little jaw muscle is moving on my jaw.

_____ Teeth are clenched together.

_____ Tongue is plastered to my teeth or roof of my mouth.

_____ Face looks drawn and tight in the mouth and/or jaw.

_____ Muscles are sore below my ears.

_____ Mouth does not open or close easily.

_____ Clicking or jerking on opening or closing mouth.

_____ **Total Score**

What's Your Score?

Now add up your score. Did you mark off more than one? Then it's important for you to read this chapter. If you didn't mark off any, read this chapter anyway. Everybody needs to learn proper breathing for anger release and relaxation. Also, if you live in an area where there's pollution, or if you live or work in a stressful atmosphere, you will need to do this breathing.

Everybody needs to learn proper breathing for anger release and relaxation.

Removing Lockjaw

Close your lips and put your hands on your cheeks along your teeth line. Keep your lips together and drop your jaw, just let it open. The top teeth should not be anywhere near the bottom teeth! Just let it sag. Let your fingers find the space between your top teeth and bottom teeth. Does it feel strange? Does it hurt? Is it an effort to make your jaw stay relaxed? Does your jaw feel like it's locked in the clenched-teeth position? It is so important to relax your jaw every minute you are awake and just before going to sleep. This one exercise alone can prevent tension in your body and not let anger build up.

Ping-Pong Anyone?

Just imagine you have a ping-pong ball inside your mouth. Now try it: Open your mouth wide enough to hold a ping-pong ball. Your teeth should be separated, your tongue should lie flat on the floor of your mouth, and the back of your tongue should be relaxed and down to make room for that ball.

The Big Chew

Open your mouth really wide. Try to get the corners of your mouth to touch your ears; let your chin touch your chest. Now that's really open big.

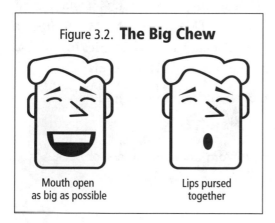

Figure 3.2. **The Big Chew**

Mouth open as big as possible

Lips pursed together

Close your mouth and purse your lips together in a moue (a puckering grimace). Squeeze your lips so tight you couldn't even put a cocktail straw in them. Open up big again. Do this over and over a few more times like you are chewing really big. That's why I call this exercise the Big Chew. (See Figure 3.2.)

This exercise will relax your jaw, cheeks, lips, and face. It can even help to prevent or reverse sagging skin in your face. It is excellent to reduce jaw tension. You can do this at your desk, in the checkout line at the supermarket, on the bus or subway, or in your car on the way to or from work. Do it as often as you can to release jaw tension.

The Rolling Chew

"I saw you on TV doing that Big Chew exercise. You looked silly, but I tried it anyway," Margaret wrote in a letter to me. "I can't believe how much more relaxed I feel."

I once did a segment on the Canadian national TV show *Live It Up* on using exercises instead of a surgical facelift. The Big Chew was part of it. So was the Rolling Chew. For this jaw-releasing tension tamer you just pucker up real tight and make circles with the pucker at the same time that you chew. Work your tongue and teeth like you are chewing and keep the pucker. To help you make circles, imagine that your face is a clock and place the pucker at 12 o'clock. Then go to 3 o'clock, 6 o'clock, 9 o'clock, and back to 12 o'clock. Of course your jaw will move and you'll want to keep your teeth apart. Eventually you will get good at this and be able to do it anywhere, anytime. The principle behind this exercise is that sometimes it's essential to tighten up muscles before they will release and relax.

TMJ Release

People pay a lot of money to get a devise to wear on their teeth so their jaw hinge (temporomandibular joint or TMJ) isn't tight. Many times a tight TMJ can lead to all kinds of neck, head, and tooth injuries in addition to anger buildup. Here are some symptoms of TMJ problems:

• Clicking or popping when you open and/or close your mouth

• Pain in the jaw, mainly the TMJ

• Pain that radiates from the TMJ to your neck, shoulders, or back

• Headache

• Toothache

• Sore jaw muscles from chewing

• Inability to completely open the jaw[1]

Doctors now talk about temporal mandibular dysfunction (TMD). You can release your jaw yourself so you won't ever develop TMD by practicing three exercises described above: Removing Lockjaw, the Big Chew, and the Rolling Chew.

I had a friend in Wayne State University in Detroit who was a locally known jazz musician. He would say things like, "He's so bent out of shape about los–

ing his girlfriend his jaws are tight," or, "His jaws are so tight he can't even smoke free cigarettes." We used to laugh at some of his jaws–are–tight expressions, but I realize now it was the beginning of my understanding of tension and stress management. Of course, in the 1960s who had ever heard of stress, let alone stress management! Hans Selye didn't even publish his first book on stress until the 1970s.

Tongue on the Floor

A more advanced relaxation exercise is to put your tongue on the floor of your mouth. That's where it should always be resting. The tip of your tongue should touch lightly against the bottom of the back of your front teeth. The sides of your tongue should be resting gently against the base of your molars. No part of your tongue should be touching your teeth, just the gums. The back of your tongue should be flat. Your entire tongue should be flat. The inside of your mouth should be hollow—just a big empty space. You should actually feel like you have enough room for a ping-pong ball inside your mouth. That's what it feels like when you have your lips together/teeth apart.

ONLY WHEN YOU EAT OR TALK

There are only a few times each day when your tongue and jaw should move—when you eat or talk. That's it. All the rest of the time your jaw and tongue should be very still. Train your jaw and tongue to be still and you'll train yourself to be stress-free. That should be your ultimate goal in life: to be stress-free. Of course, that will help make you anger-free.

Chewing Gum Is for Wimps

I recommend that you never chew gum of any kind. It's really bad for your digestion and keeps your jaw and tongue moving all the time, which might make you tired from using all that excess energy. However, if you must chew gum, then you should know that you need lips together/teeth apart even more than most people. Often people chew gum to try to balance their TMJ. When you have tension that you hold in your jaw and/or neck, you might be trying to release it by constantly chewing gum. Bruxism (teeth grinding) is also a way the body has of trying to release tension and/or trying to balance the teeth. If your teeth are not balanced, which could be due to faulty dental work, loss of a filling or tooth surface, or jaw tension, you might also grind your teeth to try to balance the teeth. Seeing a dentist is a better choice.

Why is chewing gum so bad for you? Because it causes your digestion to get out of balance. Each time you chew, your body gets a signal that food is coming and it produces the required digestive materials and movements. If you chew gum and don't eat food, what will all those digestive enzymes do? Eventually the stomach can get so mixed up that when food actually is eaten, there won't be any digestive material secreted to digest it. When your digestion isn't working properly, you won't be able to absorb the very nutrients from your food or supplements that you need to help you relax. And you won't be healthy enough to withstand stress (see Chapter 4). Please don't chew gum, not even sugar-free gum.

PUMP THE BELLOWS

Your body contains a very effective bellows. It is called your diaphragm. This is the muscle that works your lungs. It is the most important muscle in your body. Without it, you wouldn't be able to breathe. And yet, for most people, it is one of the least used muscles in the body. In the Western world we learn to hold our breath and/or do shallow breathing very early in life. Shallow breathing can lead to panic attacks, fear, lack of confidence, and in some cases even death. Older people, people under stress, people with anger, rage, or blood sugar problems all do shallow breathing. Often people go into anger and rage mode to get more oxygen into their bodies, all because of shallow breathing. Using your diaphragm—pumping the bellows—can restore vitality to your body and mind. You will look and feel younger if you get the most oxygen into your brain as possible. Deep breathing, full breathing, will do this.

> "My son fell down the stairs and I started to panic," my student related to me after yoga class. "But I remembered to do the deep breathing and it calmed me down. I could help him instead of succumbing to the usual panic attacks I have."

Where Is This Muscle?

The diaphragm is a large muscle that covers your entire body from front to back and from side to side around the area of your belly button. Actually it's the muscle that jumps when you cough and sneeze or when you have hiccups or diaphragmatic spasms. You also use your diaphragm when you pant. You have used it to do all these things without even knowing it.

All mammals have a diaphragm; your dog and cat each have one, too. Only they use theirs all the time. Just take a look at a dog after he's been playing or running, and he flops down and starts doing a panting breathing routine. His diaphragm is moving in and out to work his lungs and restore oxygen to his body and brain.

It's Like a Drum Skin

If you could look at your diaphragm when it's relaxed and not working at all, it would look like a drum skin. If you could saw your body in half, one half might be covered with the diaphragm and look exactly like the top of a drum. That's how big the muscle is. It's attached to your ribs at each side, on your front near the navel, and on your back about waist-high near your spine.

Check Out Your Ribs

Put your hands on your chest just below the breastbone where the ribs start. Feel down your ribs on each side with your fingers. The ribs go almost to your waist. Wherever you have ribs, you have lungs underneath. Bet you never thought of that before.

Check Out Your Diaphragm

Below your lungs is your diaphragm, which has three main positions: inhale, exhale, and resting (see Figure 3.3 on page 50). When you inhale, your diaphragm is supposed to drop down into your abdominal body cavity. It looks like a big salad bowl. This allows the lungs to expand and take in air. When you exhale, the diaphragm is supposed to go up into your upper chest cavity. It looks like an inverted salad bowl. This squeezes all

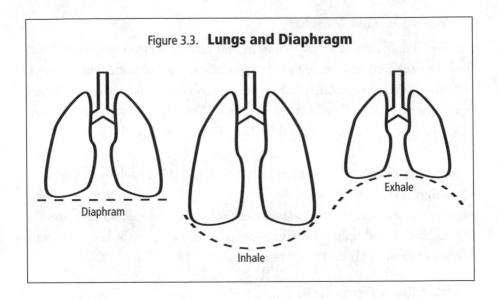

Figure 3.3. **Lungs and Diaphragm**

the air out of your lungs. In the resting position the diaphragm is completely flat. This happens when you don't breathe at all. Often as you prepare to hold your breath or do something strenuous, you inhale first so the
diaphragm should be like a big salad bowl. Your tummy and/or waist
should move when you breathe. That's an indication you're doing the correct breathing. Your shoulders have very little to do with correct breathing
and should not move at all when you breathe. Just look at the diagrams to
see what correct diaphragmatic breathing should look like.

When I taught yoga, I discovered that most people didn't use their
diaphragm for breathing unless they were exerting themselves, running
up the stairs, or playing sports. North Americans are so used to shallow
breathing that the Food and Drug Administration (FDA) has approved a
device to teach people to do slow, deep breathing to lower their blood
pressure. It often takes weeks, even months, for people to train themselves
to use their diaphragm to do the proper breathing.

USE YOUR NOSE

"Don't breathe through your mouth. It'll make your brain go soft," our school-
bus driver used to say.

"You should know," we all responded.

The best breathing is only through your nose. Your nose filters the air so it doesn't allow pollution to enter your lungs directly. The hairs in your nose trap the dust particles and keep them from going into your lungs. The hairs in your nose and your nasal passage warm the air as it passes through so cold air doesn't enter your lungs directly. In the winter your nose warms the air so the cold air doesn't shock your lungs. If you live in a cold or polluted area, if you have allergies, if you want strength, if you want to be vital and alert, breathe through your nose only, especially when you are outside.

> *It is essential to your very survival to breathe with your diaphragm and through your nose at all times.*

Breathing through your nose all the time can help prevent colds, allergies, and stuffy nose problems and it can help clear your head. It is essential to your very survival to breathe with your diaphragm and through your nose at all times. That is why you have a nose and a diaphragm; use them. I don't think breathing through your mouth will make your brain go soft, but it sure will make a lot of things go wrong.

TRY THESE EXERCISES

Put your hand flat on your tummy just above the navel. What do you feel? Is it moving there at all? It should be. Now become proactive with your breathing. Press your hand into your navel region a little bit and exhale, or breathe out. Then take in a big breath through your nose and let your diaphragm expand so that it pushes your hand out. Try it again and again until you get it right. If you want to see what it looks or feels like, look in a mirror and sneeze or cough. Put your hands on your waist at each side of your body with your thumbs up, palms against your waist. Feel your lower ribs working—expanding as you inhale and contracting as you exhale.

If you have trouble finding your diaphragm, do the Cough Test. Pretend you are coughing and put your hand on the front of your waist area so you can feel your diaphragm working. Coughing uses your diaphragm. So does sneezing.

Putting It All Together

Lie down on the floor on your back. Put something on your belly but-ton that you can see but that's light like a large box of facial tissues. Using your diaphragm, breathe out through your nose and watch the box go down. Inhale through your nose using your diaphragm and watch the box rise up underneath your diaphragm. Do this until you can easily move the box as you breathe. This is not a case of letting the diaphragm move the box by itself. You must use your breathing muscle to expand and contract so the box rises and falls as you breathe. Remember: Keep your lips together and your teeth apart.

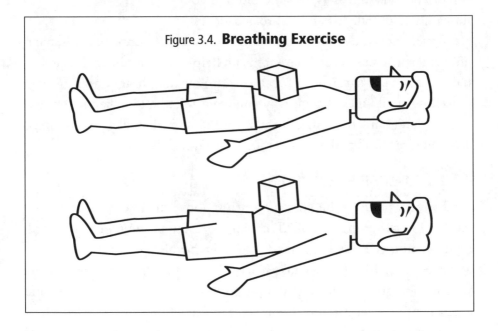

Figure 3.4. **Breathing Exercise**

ALERT, AWAKE, AWARE

Alert, awake, aware—that's what you need to be when you're in charge of your life. Be alert: Check on your breathing at different times during the day and night. Be awake: Know how to breathe properly and see if you are. Be aware: Make sure you're breathing correctly. Take time every day to be alert, awake, and aware of your breathing. The more you are aware of your breathing and begin to correct it, the more energy you'll have.

REVERSE STRESS

Stress can make your breathing become shallow, thereby depriving your body and brain of much-needed nutrients. Deep, correct breathing can reverse the tension caused by shallow breathing. If you are under stress, do the deep breathing using your diaphragm and you will soon find yourself becoming relaxed and confident. Deep breathing brings fresh oxygen to all parts of your body, giving you strength and clarity of mind. Oxygen is essential for relaxation.

Anger can also create stress so when you release stress through deep breathing, you release anger as well. If you are constantly under stress and your breathing is shallow, you may constantly have high blood pressure as well.

LOWER YOUR BLOOD PRESSURE

In 2005 a company began advertising a "machine" that they said was guaranteed and approved by the FDA to lower blood pressure without drugs. The advertisements said that breathing fewer than ten breaths a minute would lower blood pressure.

People who do yoga, tai chi, and Pilates have known this for years. Slow, deep breathing is relaxing and can help lower stress and blood pressure. Since part of the stress (fight-or-flight) response is to make your breathing shallow, it stands to reason that slow, deep breathing can reverse the response—*and* lower your blood pressure.

Many people over forty-five years of age have gotten into the habit of breathing in short, quick, shallow breaths. This is a great way to develop high blood pressure and create an environment in your body that is conducive to angry outbursts. If this applies to you, please practice slow, deep breathing as described below.

> Bill approached me at a trade show to see if, as a nutritionist, I knew a way to lower his high blood pressure. I taught him to breathe slowly from his diaphragm. He did it for three minutes and lowered his blood pressure for several hours. His circulation improved and his complexion became pink and rosy instead of gray and pasty. Bill decided to practice slow, deep breathing every day to help control his high blood pressure.

Special Blood-Pressure-Lowering Breathing

Sit in a comfortable chair with your lower back supported and feet flat on the floor. Inhale, using your diaphragm as described earlier in this chapter, for four seconds and exhale for four seconds. Count in your mind—one alligator, two alligator, three alligator, four alligator—then exhale to the same count. Do this for a few minutes and then increase the count to five seconds each on the inhale and the exhale. Do that for a few minutes. Practice this until you can do a count of six or more. Always do the same count for inhale and exhale and only breathe through your nose.

"I was starting to get uptight in a traffic jam. I could feel it building to an angry blowup. Then I remembered to do the slow, deep, diaphragmatic breathing. I did it and was calm in just a few minutes. I arrived home relaxed, not my usual cranky self." Toby was learning to keep calm and reduce her anger response.

BREATHING FOR STRENGTH

When you want more strength in your body, practice using your breath to get it. When you use your diaphragm to control your breath, you will also control the amount of strength you have. Have you ever noticed that weight lifters use very specific deep breathing to be able to lift weights? When you are trying to loosen a jar lid, use controlled, slow exhalation breathing while turning the lid and you will have more strength and success. The power of your diaphragm is amazing once you harness it.

Breath Control

When I lived in Toronto, I used to run up the subway stairs. By using breath control, I was refreshed by the time I got to the top. The people who were plodding along were worn out by the time they got there.

If you want to run up a flight of stairs and not be panting or exhausted when you get to the top, control your breathing. Practice this a lot and you will increase your lung capacity, too. Start before you get to the stairs. Inhale a complete breath, letting your diaphragm drop down into the floor of your abdomen. As you mount the stairs, do very controlled, slow breathing. Measure it by counting the stairs. To begin, inhale for the count of six stairs and exhale for the count of six stairs. Then increase the count as you get more proficient. Inhale for ten and exhale for ten. And so on. By the time you get to the top, you will be refreshed and vital.

Don't let going up stairs drain your energy and make you tired. Use everything you do to remind yourself to use breathing as a strengthening force in your life. Breathing is life to your body and brain. Practice measured breathing anytime you're walking.

> *Breathing is life to your body and brain. Practice measured breathing anytime you're walking.*

Step Count

Once you have the basic diaphragmatic breathing down and it feels normal, you can add in walking breathing. There's nothing wrong with putting your hand on your midsection to check your breathing while you walk. You can even put your hands on your lower ribs to see if they are expanding as you inhale and contracting as you exhale.

Now pick a step count, starting with six. Inhale while you are taking six steps and exhale while you are taking six steps. Do this for several blocks just to get used to measured breathing. Then do the advanced step count: double your steps on the exhale. Six steps on the inhale and twelve steps while you exhale. Do this for several more blocks. Gradually increase your breaths to eight, ten, and so forth.

Practice the step count wherever you go. For example, park in the farthest place in the shopping center parking lot and do the step count to the store. Even in the grocery store do it as you go up and down the aisles. That is the perfect place to practice a relaxation technique if there ever was one.

You will get less tired, less stressed out, and feel more alert and vital if you do this breathing everywhere you walk. If you use walking to feed your body and brain with life-giving oxygen, you'll start to have fewer aches and pains and more vitality. You might even begin to feel younger! Deep breathing and walking techniques can help improve your mood and prevent you from flying off the handle or getting mad at yourself or someone else. Keep your lips together and teeth apart.

Extreme Breathing

A very popular breathing technique for vitality, weight loss, and general well-being comes from several different traditions like yoga, chi gong, tai chi, Pilates, and breathing for weight loss programs. It's called Extreme Breathing. (Note: If you have any health problems, please check with your doctor before doing this technique.) You inhale through your nose, keeping your diaphragm tight as you inhale, taking in as much air as you can. (Don't move your shoulders.) Then exhale through your nose or pursed lips until all the air is gone. Do that by squeezing your diaphragm and lifting it until all your organs are contracted, even your abdomen and lower ribs. Keep contracting until all the air is gone. Then hold your breath out for a few seconds and slowly inhale through your nose or pursed lips until you have expanded your lower ribs, waist, diaphragm, and upper abdomen. When your lungs are full, hold the air in for a few seconds and then exhale using your diaphragm. I like to use the count of six in, hold for six, exhale for twelve, and hold out for six. Once you are comfortable with that, increase the count to eight and sixteen, ten and twenty, and so on.

Extreme Contraction

Once you get really good at Extreme Breathing, you can go on to Extreme Contraction. (This is called by different names in different systems, but I like to call it Extreme Contraction.) Do Extreme Breathing, and when you have completely exhaled, pull your diaphragm up toward your heart and hold it without breathing. In yoga this is called *uddiyana,* which means to fly up. It is a lock, or *bandha,* that is used for strengthening the diaphragm. When you get really good, you can pull your diaphragm up and pump it while holding your breath out. Check with any qualified yoga teacher for instructions.

IMPROVE YOUR MOOD

Deep breathing and exercises like walking are known to improve your mood and give you a more positive outlook on life. It is more difficult for someone to make you mad if you have a positive attitude or good self-esteem.

The old adage of counting to ten before you yell or get mad at someone is a great idea. Especially if you do deep breathing and jaw-releasing techniques while you count to ten. You might be able to defuse the reaction and anger completely. Try it and see if you feel better, have fewer outbursts, and enjoy life more because you are more relaxed.

CHAPTER SUMMARY

1. Lips together/teeth apart and tongue flat—do that relaxation and stress management exercise every day wherever you are.

2. The Big Chew and the Rolling Chew exercises release face and neck tension.

3. Avoid chewing gum.

4. Use your diaphragm for breathing. Always breathe through your nose.

5. Deep breathing and breath control give you relaxation and strength.

CHAPTER 4

Chew on This

"I can't for the life of me figure out how you ate that whole senior omelet without drinking any water," the overweight waiter said with his Southern drawl. *"I chewed it!"* was my reply.

He was young and big—huge, in fact. I'm not sure who was more shocked: the young man, who always washed his food down with ice water, or me, the chewing-fanatic nutritionist who couldn't believe her ears!

Did you know that in North America most people don't chew their food? They simply wash it down with ice water, coffee, or soft drinks. They are committing two of the deadliest "sins" known to humankind:

1. Not chewing their food. (That's why they have to wash it down.)

2. Drinking ice water or other iced liquids with meals (or anytime for that matter).

CHEWING STARTS DIGESTION

Chewing starts digestion! That's a simple fact of how your body works. That phrase, one of my favorites, has gotten me in more trouble than anything else I ever say. Once when I was the official nutritionist for the local Toronto CBC-Radio show called *The 4 to 6 Show,* I used it as one of my regular features and I received complaints from somebody with the registered dietitians' association. The person jumped all over me for saying it until I pointed out that my source was a high school textbook written by well-known and well-respected doctors at the largest children's hospital in Canada. The trouble stopped right away.

Yes, it's true: chewing starts digestion. The more you chew each mouthful of food, the better you will digest it. Acupuncturists tell me there are points of stimulation under all the teeth that start digestion. That applies whether you have natural teeth, implants, or false teeth. Each time you chew food, you tell your body to start the process of digestion. Studies show that chewing starches actually infuses them with the very enzyme needed to digest them.

When you don't chew your food before you swallow it, you're asking for several different kinds of trouble in your body. Allergies, acid reflux, indigestion, stomach and intestinal troubles, headaches, constipation, diarrhea, frequent colds, and a lot of immune and autoimmune diseases can be directly traced back to not chewing your food or to poor digestion.

TAKE THE DIGESTION TEST

You're probably thinking you don't need to read this chapter. *But you do*. Every chapter in *The Anger Cure* is specifically designed to help you diagnose your habits and lifestyle so that you can choose to have the best health possible.

I have never met anybody in the 250,000 or so people I have done nutrition education programs with who had efficient digestion. So take the Digestion Test and see if you have problems.

THE GREAT IMPOSTER

Gum is the great imposter. When you chew gum, you confuse your digestion. Just imagine how it appears from the standpoint of your stomach:

"Wow, he's eating something. I better get ready," says the stomach. So it starts to secrete stomach acid and begins to churn in preparation for some food.

"I wonder when he's going to swallow that stuff? I've been ready for ten minutes. Oh, I don't feel so good. All that stomach acid and no food to use it up."

DIGESTION TEST

Mark off all that apply to you. Give yourself 1 point for each mark.

_____ Loss of taste for meat

_____ Bad breath

_____ Gas shortly after eating

_____ Frequent belching

_____ Coated tongue (especially in the morning)

_____ A lot of foul-smelling gas

_____ Indigestion (can be as soon as a half hour after eating or up to four hours after eating)

_____ Acid reflux (sour-tasting liquid coming up into the throat or mouth)

_____ Burning stomach sensations that eating relieves

_____ Mucus colitis (now called irritable bowel syndrome)

_____ Bloating in the stomach or abdominal region

_____ Lower bowel gas (especially several hours after eating)

_____ Heartburn

_____ **Total Score**

What's Your Score?

The only passing score for this one is zero. That's right: nada, zilch. If you have a mark next to any of the items, it's an indication you have digestion problems. But if your score shows that digestion is not an issue for you, skip to the next chapter. However, I don't believe you. I have never met a person with good or proper digestion!

When chewing gum is a regular habit, how will your stomach know whether to prepare for food or not? So your stomach says, "I guess I'll just get used to making less stomach acid. That way I'll be safe. He won't be able to digest as well, but at least I won't hurt myself." Chewing gum throws off your digestive ability. Now that you know that, isn't it time you stopped using the Great Imposter?

THE SHOCK OF ICE

Ice, ice water, and iced drinks all shock your stomach. Yes, it's a major shock to your system when your normal body temperature is 98.6°F and you consume something that's frozen. The temperature of iced drinks is about 37 to 48°F. That quick temperature change can be very stressful, and stress stops digestion as part of the fight-or-flight response. (This is covered in Chapters 7 and 8.) So that means every time you drink ice-cold drinks you're causing stress and, thereby, reducing your ability to digest.

> "Would you like something to drink?" the waitress asked. "No, nothing," was my reply. A few minutes later she arrived at my table with water that had ice in it!
> "I said nothing to drink."
> "But you can't eat without having something to drink," was her reply.

It's the American Way

In North America most people wash their food down with some kind of cold liquid. But would you do that if you knew it was a great way to get fat?

THE APPESTAT AND WEIGHT LOSS

When I was leading "The Tofu Whole Foods Weight-Loss Program: The Diet of the Stars" class in Toronto many years ago, several people said they didn't know how much to eat. I suspected they weren't chewing their food so I asked them to sit in a circle with me in the middle. I gave them pieces of whole-wheat pita bread and asked them to chew it and to raise their hands when they were ready to swallow it. Then I looked in their mouths. Every one of them was about to swallow a piece of food that still looked like a piece of pita bread! I realized they were nearly inhaling their food completely unchewed. This never gave them a chance to feel full or to properly digest their food.

When you chew food thoroughly, your brain has a better chance of knowing when you're full so you don't eat too much and you digest what you eat. It takes about twenty minutes from the time you've actually eaten enough until your brain tells you to stop eating. That internal mechanism is like a thermostat that measures your hunger or appetite. That's why it's called "the appestat." When you chew each mouthful until it is liquid, you will spend more time chewing and less time taking in food so you will naturally be in sync with the twenty-minute delay and not eat too much. Your appestat will work better.

So if you want to lose weight—or just be healthy—the very first thing to change is how you chew and how much you chew each mouthful. The more you chew each mouthful, the better you will digest it and the more nutrition you will get out of it. So it follows that you will eat less. In this case less is more.

LIQUID FOOD

If you want to be healthy, you will concentrate on chewing each mouthful until it is completely liquid in your mouth. Do not swallow it sooner. Do not wash the food down with a liquid. If you chew your food thoroughly, it will go down easily. Just like in the old proverb: "Let your food be your liquid and your liquid be your food."

LESS FOOD (MORE CHEWING) = MORE ABSORPTION

STARCH DIGESTER

All starch begins to be digested with the saliva in your mouth. This means that to really digest starch—peas, potatoes, lima beans, corn, bread, wheat, rice, oats, grains, fruit, and anything made of them—you will need to chew it well. The ptyalin, also called amylase, in your saliva helps to digest starches of all kinds. So the more you chew starches the easier they are to digest.

CHEWING TEST

Take the Chewing Test. Put a piece of food in your mouth. Please use real food like whole grains, fresh vegetables, or protein. Count the number of times you chew the mouthful. Start by counting the number of times you would normally chew it and write that down. Swallow the food. Now take another bite and chew it for ten times. How was that? Was it difficult? Is it really chewed enough? Are ten chews more than you chew each mouthful normally? Keep going; take another mouthful and chew it twenty times. That may be more difficult. Health experts say we should chew each mouthful fifty times! Who has that amount of time to eat? Who has that kind of patience? You should. I should. We all should.

RESULTS OF POOR DIGESTION

The minister's hair was snowy white and he was only in his forties. Then it started to grow in darker. I suspected supplements. Yes, someone had gotten him on a very complete vitamin and mineral supplement that contained all the vitamins, minerals, and digestive enzymes. And his halitosis began to subside as well.

Poor digestion can cause premature aging. This is the number-one reason to improve your digestion!

Poor digestion can cause all kinds of health problems, not just digestive disturbances. Faulty digestion can often bring on chronic fatigue,

Digestion Information

- Chewing breaks down the actual food.

- Saliva starts the digestion of starches.

- Chewing starts the digestion process.

- Hunks of swallowed food can suppress your immune function.

- Undigested foods in the stomach can cause stress.

- Stress of all kinds stops digestion.*

  * See Chapter 2, The Hidden Killer of Relationships and Love; Chapter 7, How Your Body Creates Anger; and Chapter 8, Anger and the Fight-or-Flight Response.

arthritis, poor skin and hair quality, allergies, cancer,[1] and reduced immune function. When your body is under this kind of stress, it's also easy to feel bad about yourself. This makes you more susceptible to anger and rage. Poor digestion can also throw your blood sugar out of balance, which can trigger anger, rage, and violence.

Gray hair can be a sign of poor digestion. Here's why: The minerals zinc and copper and the B vitamin PABA are most responsible for preventing gray hair. If you cannot break them down or absorb them because of poor digestion, you may have gray hair. Now if you haven't eaten any foods or taken supplements containing these nutrients, then digestion isn't even a part of the picture. You can't break down and absorb what you haven't ingested. No amount of digestive enzymes will be able to help you.

STRESS STOPS DIGESTION

Part of the stress response, called the fight-or-flight response, causes digestion to stop. This is explained more fully in Chapters 7 and 8. Every time you experience any stress—no matter how small—you must remember to chew your food to start digestion again. Or you might want to take a supplement that contains all the essentials for good digestion.

STRESS STOPS DIGESTION—CHEWING STARTS DIGESTION

STRANGE SYMPTOMS

In *The World's Oldest Health Plan*[2] I wrote that allergists thought unchewed or partially digested foods could cause allergies. That was in 1993. Now we know why. At first I thought it was just the strain of trying to digest food that wasn't fully chewed. Now I know it's part of a much bigger problem. It is called floating immune complex (FIC) or leaky gut syndrome because partially chewed or partially digested food gets into the bloodstream. The immune system thinks these particles are foreign invaders and begins to attack them.

While your immune system is thus occupied, it can't get rid of real foreign invaders like viruses, germs, or parasites. Your immunity is weakened and you may begin to have all kinds of symptoms of poor immune function. It could be just simple colds and bouts of the flu. It could be allergies. Or it could even be typical immune and autoimmune problems. The most common signs of impaired immune function include fatigue, listlessness, repeated infections, inflammations, allergic reactions, chronic diarrhea, bouts of thrush or candidiasis, and vaginal yeast infections.[3] Many immune and autoimmune diseases may well start with poor digestion. No one can say.

SUPPLEMENT WITH DIGESTIVE ENZYMES

If you are free of stress, chew each mouthful until it is liquid, relax when you eat, and still have faulty digestion, then you might want to consider taking a digestion supplement. A really good one might contain a mixture of the ingredients in Table 4.1.

TABLE 4.1. DIGESTIVE AIDS	
INGREDIENT (ENZYME)	WHAT IT DIGESTS
Protease	Protein
Amylase	Starch
Lipase	Fat
Lactase	Milk or lactose
Galactosidase	Beans, broccoli, sulfur-containing foods
Cellulase	Vegetable fibers
Sucrase	Sugar
Maltase	Sugar
Other useful ingredients: bromelain, betain, HCL (hydrochloric acid), papain.	

Even though I'm a slow eater because I chew each mouthful until it's liquid, I also take digestive enzymes—the Anger Cure Digestion Formula, of course. I do that because it isn't always possible to get the organically grown, high-nutrition raw vegetables, fruits, meats, and grains I like to eat. All natural foods contain the enzymes necessary for digesting them if they are grown with care and freshly picked. But once food is shipped any distance, the enzymes in it start to break down. Raw meat contains the enzymes needed to digest it as well, but it is almost impossible to safely eat raw meat and fish anymore because of the health problems associated with them. And those vital enzymes are really depleted during processing and storage. So that means I must take digestive enzymes to help digest everything I eat, even if I do chew thoroughly.

Enzymes Are Essential

Enzymes are essential for every function in your body. When you close your eyes, enzymes enable you to do it. When your heart beats, enzymes enable you to do it. When you think, enzymes enable you to do it. Everything that happens in your body uses enzymes. Enzymes come from food, and your body produces enzymes. There are more than 3,000 kinds of enzymes in your body. They renew, maintain, and protect all humans. You must continually supply your body with the enzymes needed to function or you will not be healthy. That is why I take enzymes even though I try to chew thoroughly.

"I used to have acid reflux disease," said George excitedly. "It was so bad I couldn't lie down to sleep, I had to sleep sitting up. When I started eating small, frequent meals and taking a mixed digestive enzyme supplement, I began to have less and less acid reflux. Even the doctor couldn't do this for me."

Heartburn, Indigestion, and Other Digestive Disturbances

There are many lifestyle choices you might be making that cause heartburn, indigestion, and other digestive upsets. (Those choices are discussed in Chapters 7 and 8.) Natural doctors and other practitioners have a much different idea about what causes these digestive problems than do the drug companies. Low enzymes! Yes, that's correct. We know that low or no enzymes are really the problem in most cases of heartburn, indigestion, and acid reflux disease.

Low or no enzymes are really the problem in most cases of heartburn, indigestion, and acid reflux disease.

Years ago I learned that the valves that open and close the stomach are kept in shape by B vitamins. Catching this early (by examining children's tongues) can prevent acid reflux. Given that poor digestion or low stomach acid can keep the stomach from emptying in a timely manner, it's obvious that the correct B vitamins in your diet and proper digestion play a huge role in preventing this problem.

When a person who has heartburn, acid reflux, or indigestion on a regular basis does not change his or her lifestyle to include the Anger Cure diet and lifestyle plan, a lot of negative results can occur, especially if the person takes antacids. Since digestive enzymes are essential for breaking down minerals during digestion, if you take antacids and neutralize your digestive enzymes, you can prevent your body from getting calcium, along with most other minerals. Calcium, along with magnesium, is essential for relaxation. Relaxation is useful to improve deep breathing and help prevent anger.

Osteoporosis and Digestion

A double-blind trial of elderly women taking the popular "ulcer" drug omeprazole (Prilosec), which was reported in 2005 in the *American Journal of Medicine,* showed two things: one, that excess stomach acid is no longer considered the cause of ulcers, and two, that reducing the amount of stomach acid with omeprazole reduced the absorption of important nutrients, including calcium, iron, and vitamin B_{12}, all of which are essential for health in older adults. The researchers' conclusions were that taking this acid blocker could contribute to anemia and other health problems and render the women more susceptible to bacterial or fungal overgrowth in their stomach or intestines. Researchers also noted that reduced calcium intake and absorption have been associated with increased risk of bone fractures, bone loss, and osteoporosis.[4]

Tying It All Together

Here's how it all ties together. When you eat a meal and you have low digestive enzymes, the food has to stay in your stomach for a lot longer than it should. All that time your stomach is working very hard to digest the food, but it doesn't have the proper amount or correct kinds of enzymes to digest it. Because you are low in enzymes, you will not be able to break down and absorb the B complex vitamins in your food or supplements. B vitamins are known to help digest carbohydrates and keep the valves at the top of the stomach toned so they open and close properly.

While the food is churning in your stomach trying to be digested, it gives off gases. These gases escape out of the stomach and up into your esophagus, taking some of the partially digested food with it. That's why you get a sour or acidy taste in your mouth when you burp. Other times the acid just goes up a little way, causing erosion of the esophagus, and never gets as far up as the back of your throat. This is called acid reflux disease. Digestive enzymes really help get most people's stomachs working again. (However, if you are under your doctor's care for any kind of digestive disturbance, please do not take digestive enzymes without his or her knowledge.)

CHAPTER SUMMARY

1. Chewing starts digestion. It is important to chew each mouthful until it is liquid in your mouth for excellent digestion. This can help balance your weight and your immune system.

2. Chewing gum and drinking ice-cold drinks are bad for your digestion and can contribute to stress.

3. Stress stops your digestion.

4. Taking digestive enzymes can improve your health, reverse aging, and help prevent anger.

5. Many digestive disturbances can be helped with digestive enzymes.

CHAPTER 5

Are You Hardening Your Heart?

Myrna called me all excited one Monday. She had been taking a class on nutrition and the Bible from me at a big church in our town. "You won't believe what happened on Saturday," she gushed. "Well, maybe you would. You are the one who told me about it. My husband and I were going shopping about 11 A.M., and we were arguing on the way to the car. As I put my hand on the door handle, I heard your voice saying in the back of my mind, "If you don't eat something and try to make your body work, you can have all kinds of strange things go wrong, including arguing and anger." I realized we hadn't eaten yet and we'd been out of bed for four hours or more. So we went back inside and ate something. The arguing stopped. Now we are going to always make sure we eat before we go out so we won't argue anymore. Isn't that wonderful!"

The heart is considered the area of the body associated with love. When you are in love, you generally feel it in your chest near the heart. This is why hearts are used to connote love of all kinds. St. Valentine's Day is all about love, and hearts figure hugely in this holiday. It stands to reason that if you want to be negative toward somebody, you would shut off your heart or harden it toward them. Many people discover in therapy that they have built a wall around their heart to keep from feeling or loving. It's a protective mechanism. It's a learned behavior, a conscious or unconscious action.

IT'S NOT JUST YOUR HEART

Many lifestyle actions will also harden your heart or the arteries around it. Anger is a big one! In the 1970s doctors and nutritionists were all talking about the new book on heart problems called *Type A Behavior and Your Heart*. This book by Meyer Friedman, M.D., and Ray H. Rosenman (Knopf, 1974; it's now out of print, but you may be able to find it in a library or secondhand bookstore) was a startling look into emotions and heart disease. It outlined a personality type that they called "type A." Their premise was that people who exhibited type A behavior had more heart attacks.

Some of the characteristics of type A behavior included: talking and walking fast, finishing other people's sentences for them, getting irritated at delays, trying to do more than one thing at once, feeling guilty if you took time off to relax, and getting angry often. As a type A at the time, I couldn't imagine being a type B who didn't do any of these things. Well, that was in the 1970s, and I've learned a lot since then.

They Called It Type A

Since the 1970s we've come to realize that the one thing that does cause heart disease in the type A behavior pattern is *anger*. How fitting that they called it type A! Years of research have shown that anger can trigger all kinds of physical problems.

We Call It Syndrome X

In 1988 Dr. Gerald M. Reaven, a Stanford University researcher, coined the term Syndrome X. After twenty years of research into insulin resistance he realized a cluster of symptoms are related to heart problems and blood sugar problems. Because he wasn't sure of the connection between heart disease and diabetes, he called it Syndrome X, because X generally stands for the unknown in science and mathematics. Now it's also called insulin resistance or metabolic syndrome. The classic symptoms Dr. Raven listed were:

1. Insulin resistance and glucose intolerance

2. Obesity

3. Blood-fat abnormalities

4. Hypertension[1]

The definition of Syndrome X has since been expanded to include blood sugar problems of all kinds and heart problems of all kinds. Glucose intolerance and insulin resistance affect more than half the population of the United States and Canada. At least 55 percent of North Americans are overweight, and an estimated 50 million suffer from either hypertension or elevated blood-fat levels. That makes Syndrome X a huge problem in North America.

> *Glucose intolerance and insulin resistance affect more than half the population of the United States and Canada.*

TAKE THE SYNDROME X TEST

To see if you might have some of the symptoms of Syndrome X, take the test.

SYNDROME X TEST

Part 1: Your Family and Personal History

1. My grandparents have or had: (1 point for each Grandparent)

   adult-onset (type 2) diabetes _____

   high blood pressure _____

   heart disease or atherosclerosis ___/___

   difficulty controlling weight _____

   high fat levels in the blood _____

2. My parents have or had: (2 points for each parent)

   adult-onset (type 2) diabetes _____

   high blood pressure ___2___

   heart disease or atherosclerosis ___2___

   difficulty controlling weight ___2___

   high fat levels in the blood ___2___

3.　I have:

adult-onset (type 2) diabetes (15 points)　　　　　　　　_____

high blood pressure (4 points)　　　　　　　　　　　　　_____

heart disease or atherosclerosis (8 points)　　　　　　　　_____

difficulty controlling weight (4 points)　　　　　　　　　*4*

high fat levels in the blood (6 points)　　　　　　　　　　_____

4.　I am:　　　　　　　　　　　　　　　　　　　　　　_____

not overweight, but I do struggle to control my weight (1 point)

less than 20 pounds overweight (2 points)

20–50 pounds overweight (3 points)

51–100 pounds overweight (4 points)

more than 100 pounds overweight (6 points)

5.　I am:　　　　　　　　　　　　　　　　　　　　　*3*

between 35 and 49 years of age (1 point)

between 50 and 64 years of age (2 points)

over 65 years of age (3 points)

Total for Part 1 (possible total 67)　　　　　　　　　　*1*

Part 2:　Your Nutritional and Lifestyle Profile

6.　I eat sweets (such as candy, ice cream, pastries, or doughnuts) four or more times a week (4 points)　　　*4*

7.　I eat "fat-free" foods (such as fat-free muffins, fruit yogurt, cookies, breakfast bars) more than four times a week (2 points)　　_____

8.　I eat potato chips, pretzels, breakfast bars, granola, or ready-to-eat breakfast cereals more than three times a week (2 points)　_____

9.　I eat meals that emphasize pasta, rice, corn, or potatoes more than three times a week (2 points)　_____

10.　I eat burgers, hot dogs, fatty luncheon meats (bologna, ham, salami), bacon, sausage, French fries, or fried chicken more than three times a week (2 points)　　*2*

11.　I eat convenience food (pizza, fast-food-style Mexican, sandwiches, or snack food) more than three times a week (2 points)　*2*

12. I drink regular (non-diet) soft drinks or sweetened ice tea more than three times a week (2 points) __2__

13. I drink more than 8 ounces of undiluted fruit juice per day (1 point) _____

14. I snack between meals (1 point) __1__

15. I drink more than two cups of coffee or tea with sugar or sweetener daily (4 points) __4__

16. I often chew gum, eat mints, or hard candy (sweetened or diet) (2 points) _____

17. I often eat when I am not hungry (2 points) _____

18. I eat food high in saturated fats almost every day (2 points) __2__

19. I often snack at night (2 points) _____

20. I avoid structured exercise (2 points) __2__

21. I avoid any exercise like walking, taking stairs, housework, gardening, or playing with children or a pet (4 points) _____

22. I have been a "couch potato" for many years (3 points) __3__

Total for Part 2 (possible total 39) __22__

Part 3: Your Stress Levels

23. I am under a great deal of stress: __3__

    at my job, but not at home (2 points)

    at home, but not at work (3 points)

    at home and at work (6 points)

24. I smoke: _____

    less than 1 pack of cigarettes a day (2 points)

    between 1 and 2 packs of cigarettes a day (6 points)

    more than 2 packs of cigarettes a day (8 points)

    cigars or a pipe (3 points)

25. I drink beer or wine: __1__

    on occasion, but then pretty large amounts (2 points)

    2 or 3 times a week more than 2 glasses (1 point)

once a day, 1 or 2 glasses (0 points)

twice or more a day (5 points)

26. I drink mixed drinks: _____

on occasion, but then pretty large amounts (2 points)

2 or 3 times a week, but then more than 2 glasses (1 point)

once a day, 1 or 2 glasses (2 points)

twice or more a day (6 points)

27. I take birth control pills or female hormone replacement medication (2 points) _____

Total for Part 3 (possible total 51) *4*

Part 4: Your Symptoms

28. I often feel tired, particularly after eating lunch or dinner (1 point) *1*

29. I have difficulty concentrating (1 point) *1*

30. My thinking is frequently fuzzy or spacey (1 point) _____

31. I often get irritable or angry (1 point) *1*

32. I experience frequent cravings for sugar or other carbohydrates such as pasta, bread, or baked goods (4 points) *4*

33. I have a tendency to binge on sweets or other carbohydrates (2 points)

34. I feel shaky if I don't eat on time or if I don't get snacks (4 points) *2*

35. I have a tendency to gain weight easily and have difficulty losing it (3 points) *3*

36. I have a "pot belly" around my waist (males) (6 points) _____

37. I carry fat more in my abdominal region or upper body instead of on my hips and thighs (females) (6 points) *6*

38. I feel the need to urinate frequently (5 points) _____

39. I often have unexplained thirst (5 points) _____

Total for Part 4 (possible total 38) *18*

Total for Part 1 *2* *17*

Total for Part 2 *22*

Total for Part 3 *4*

Total for Part 4 *18*

61

Grand Total (possible total 195)

This test was given to me by one of Canada's leading clinical herbalists, Dr. Terry Willard, Cl.H., Ph.D., and used with permission.

What's Your Score?

What was your grand total? Did you score between 0 and 15? If so, you don't have a risk for Syndrome X. If you wish, you can go on to the next chapter, but you might want to read this chapter anyway because you surely know somebody in your family or a friend who has Syndrome X, and this will help you work with them.

Did you score between 16 and 25? If so, you may be in the beginning stages of insulin resistance. You need to read this chapter. Did you score between 26 and 50? You probably have insulin resistance and are heading for Syndrome X. You need a comprehensive program, including proper diet, supplements, and exercise. Keep reading. Did you score over 50? Then it's pretty definite that you have insulin resistance and Syndrome X. Keep reading and go to your doctor to test for Syndrome X.

"I just don't know what to do or who I am anymore, Kathleen," a student explained to me one night at cooking class. "Last week my four-year-old spilled her milk, and I just wiped it up and got her another cup of milk. Tonight she did the same thing, and I yelled at her. I was so angry I could have hit her. What's happening to me?"

WHAT'S ANGER GOT TO DO WITH IT?

How many of the tests so far have included anger? Anger was in the Low Blood Sugar Test and the Syndrome X Test. It will also be in another test in Chapter 6. Anger is a symptom that occurs when your body is out of balance, like my student in the case study above. Generally it occurs when your blood sugar is either too high or too low. This kind of anger is often described as getting angry unexpectedly or anger that bubbles up from nowhere, often surprising you and the recipient. Flying off the handle describes the kind of anger that comes from having low levels of serotonin, a brain chemical affected by blood sugar levels. Low levels of another brain chemical, beta-endorphin, can also give rise to anger. Aside from reducing anger when it's high, beta-endorphins also increase feelings of well-being and self-esteem as well as dispel anxiety, paranoid feelings, and depression.

Blood sugar, serotonin, and beta-endorphins are all thrown off by consumption of sugar and sugary products. This includes sweet fruits and carbohydrate foods like bread and pastries as well as alcohol.[2] No wonder there's a diet connection to anger.

THE HEART CONNECTION

Dr. Terry Willard of Wild Rose Herbal Formulas put the heart-Syndrome X connection together for me in a lecture in Toronto, Ontario, in 2000. He went so far as to say that North Americans are closing off their hearts with their dietary habits: "Sugar takes us away from being able to love and turns us more to anger." He went on to explain that the foods we eat can cause blood sugar fluctuations, which then lead to insulin sensitivity, and that starts to cause heart problems and obesity. It is also true that many of the foods the average person eats are low in B complex vitamins. B complex vitamins, especially B_6, B_{12}, and folic acid, are essential for keeping your heart functioning properly. If you eat a diet high in sugar or white flour products and don't consume any B complex vitamins, you can become deficient in B vitamins. Vitamin B_6 and pantothenic acid (often called B_5) are necessary to withstand stress, stabilize your blood sugar, and improve insulin usage. Vitamin B_1 is essential for carbohydrate metabolism. All B vitamins are needed for you to be healthy and have a healthy heart. How many B vitamin deficiency signs did you see on your tongue, lips, and hands in Chapter 1?

INSULIN AND YOUR HEART

High insulin levels, either as a result of lifestyle or from injections, can produce a greater risk for coronary heart disease, ischemic heart disease, and damage to your body from oxidized LDL cholesterol. High insulin levels can

Excess insulin levels lead to increases in body fats, blood pressure, and obesity.

also alter the linings of the blood vessels, leading to plaque buildup.[3] Excess insulin levels lead to increases in body fats (both cholesterol and triglycerides), blood pressure, and obesity. Obesity puts a strain on your heart because of the additional weight your body carries around. Keeping insulin levels stabilized is very important for the most efficient functioning of your heart.

MAKING SENSE OF IT ALL

The ideal method for eliminating anger, low self-esteem, negativity, flying off the handle, depression, obesity, and most of the items listed in the Low Blood Sugar Test and the Syndrome X Test is to avoid allowing your insulin levels to go up so high that your body can't handle them. That means avoiding the foods, beverages, and habits that raise insulin levels. In a perfect world, avoiding caffeine, nicotine, white flour products, white sugar products, and sweet foods like bananas and fruit juices, as well as starchy foods like corn, peas, potatoes, rice, and pasta, would correct the problem. This would mean eating only protein and vegetables. It would work, but it would be difficult to do all the time. You might lose your friends with a strict diet like that. The Anger Cure program is a lot easier to follow.

THE GLYCEMIC INDEX

The glycemic index (GI) is a measurement of how quickly food raises your blood sugar once you eat it. It is a simple guide for helping you plan meals. Scientists used sugar as the base and assigned it the number 100. All other foods were assigned a number depending on how much and/or how fast they each raised blood sugar levels and, therefore, insulin levels. One cup (1 ounce) of Kellogg's Corn Flakes has a GI of 87. Three quarters of a cup (1 ounce) of Kellogg's Frosted Flakes has a GI of 55. According to the GI rating, corn flakes cause a faster increase in blood sugar levels than the sweetened flakes. When you add milk, you slow the rate at which your insulin goes up because adding fat and/or protein to a high-glycemic food slows the rate at which it enters your bloodstream. To give you an idea of the glycemic index, Table 5.1 lists some common foods and their GI ratings.

TABLE 5.1. COMMON FOODS AND THEIR GLYCEMIC INDEX (GI) RATINGS

FOOD ITEM (100 GRAMS)	GI RATING	FOOD ITEM (100 GRAMS)	GI RATING
Beans		Grapenuts	67
soy	18	Shredded Wheat	69
kidney	27	Cheerios	74
red lentils	27	Puffed Wheat	74
lentil	30	Corn Bran	75
black	30	Total	76
butter	31	Grapenuts Flakes	80
split peas	32	Rice Krispies	82
baby lima	32	Team	82
chickpeas	33	Corn Chex	83
brown	38	Cornflakes	83
navy	38	Crispix	87
pinto	42	Rice Chex	89
baked	43	Puffed Rice	90
Breads		**Crackers**	
pumpernickel	49	rye	63
rye, whole	50	Kavli Norwegian	71
pita	57	saltines	72
rye	64	graham crackers	75
bagel	72	corn chips	75
white	72	water crackers	78
whole wheat	72	rice cakes	82
Kaiser roll	73	**Nuts and Seeds**	most range
waffles	76		from 15–30
Cereals		**Fruits**	
Rice Bran	19	cherries	22
All Bran	44	plum	24
oatmeal	49	grapefruit	25
Special K	54	apricot, dried	30
Frosted Flakes	55	banana, unripe	30
Bran Chex	58	strawberries	30
Swiss Muesli	60	pear	36
Cream of Wheat	66	apple	38
Life	66	peach	42
NutriGrain	66	grapes	43
oatmeal, 1 min	66	orange	43

Food Item (100 grams)	GI Rating
strawberry jam	51
kiwi	52
apricot jam	55
fruit cocktail	55
mango	50
papaya	58
banana	62
apricot, canned	64
raisins	64
cantaloupe	65
pineapple	66
watermelon	72
dates, dried	103
Grains	
barley	22
rye	34
hominy	40
whole wheat	41
bulgur	47
rice, parboiled	47
buckwheat	54
popcorn (without butter)	55
sweet corn	55
brown rice	59
couscous	65
cornmeal	68
millet	75
white rice	88
rice, instant	91
Milk Products	
soymilk	31
Milk (cow or goat)	34
chocolate milk	34
yogurt	38
pudding	43
ice cream	50

Food Item (100 grams)	GI Rating
Pasta	
spaghetti, protein enriched	28
vermicelli	35
spaghetti	40
whole-grain pasta	45
macaroni	46
linguine, durum	50
vermicelli, rice	58
macaroni and cheese	64
white flour pasta	65
gnocchi	68
brown rice pasta	92
Vegetables	
tomatoes	15
olives	18
lettuce, all types	less than 30
cauliflower	less than 30
broccoli	less than 30
eggplant	less than 30
onions	less than 30
radishes	less than 30
yellow and zucchini squash	less than 30
water chestnuts	less than 30
sauerkraut	less than 30
green beans	40
yams	50
sweet potatoes	55
corn	75
beets	75
French-fried potatoes	80
carrots	85
baked potato (without butter or sour cream)	95

If you must eat carbohydrate foods, eat those with a GI rating of 50 or less. Always eat carbohydrates with fat, fiber, protein, or something acidic like vinegar, lemon or lime juice, or sauerkraut.

There's More to It

Table 5.1 gives the GI for 100 grams of food. That is not always a serving size. As noted above, eating protein or fat in the same meal as a carbohydrate or high-GI food will slow the rate at which it raises your blood sugar levels and, therefore, your insulin levels. Many traditional ethnic recipes contain, along with carbohydrates, condiments that slow the rate at which blood sugar goes up. Lemon juice, vinegar, butter, oil, garlic, fenugreek seeds (found in many different ethnic recipes such as curry powders), and sauerkraut all lessen the GI rating of grains and starchy vegetables. "Sushi" literally means vinegared rice. When you eat traditional sushi with vinegar in the white rice, sea vegetables, and fish, you lower the GI of the meal. As soon as you add sugar in the dip or drink alcohol, you raise it.

Lemon juice, vinegar, butter, oil, garlic, fenugreek seeds, and sauerkraut all lessen the GI rating of grains and starchy vegetables.

If you want to have fruit, make sure it is low GI and sprinkle lime juice or balsamic vinegar on it to lessen the rate at which it goes into your bloodstream. You don't need to use sugar; lime juice brings out the sweetness and lowers the GI of the fruit.

"I always feel sleepy after I eat a meal. That's why I don't eat breakfast. What can I do?" This statement is typical of a person with blood sugar fluctuations. High blood sugar and/or high insulin levels can make you very sleepy. This woman was eating a sugar–coated cereal, a banana, toast and jam, and coffee with sugar for breakfast. No wonder she was sleepy.

Total Meal Count

It isn't just one food's GI rating that you need to be concerned with—it's the GI rating of the entire meal. That means having protein with all carbohydrates like breads, fruits, or pastas. If you have an apple, have a little piece of cheese with it. If you have pretzels or crackers, have unsweetened peanut or almond butter or cheese with them. In other words, don't eat high-glycemic foods by themselves. Yes, that means we're back to meat and potatoes with a salad (dressed with lemon juice or vinegar). It's a lot easier on your body to just have the meat and salad, but if you have the potatoes, don't have bread, rolls, or dessert. If you're going to have bread, make sure it's whole-grain sourdough bread and be sure to eat it with some protein and veggies. The acid used in making the sourdough helps to reduce blood sugar and insulin levels compared to non-sourdough breads. Dr. Willard told me he serves his family oatmeal for breakfast with sauerkraut on it! It took them a while to get used to it, but now they eat it.

Processing Boosts GI Rating

Generally, the more a food is processed, the more its GI rating goes up. So wheat berries have a lower GI than whole-wheat flour. Whole-wheat flour has a lower rating than white flour. So if you're eating grains, it's best to eat the entire grain with one of the slowing factors like butter, oil, lemon juice, or protein. Fried rice is a good example of how to reduce the GI rating. Fried rice usually has eggs and some other protein and oil is used in the cooking process. Low-glycemic vegetables like mushrooms, green beans, bok choy, water chestnuts, or parsley are added, and it's often seasoned with garlic.

The Framingham Offspring Study concluded that increased intake of whole grains may reduce the disease risk in type 2 diabetes and cardiovascular disease.[4] In other words whole grains can even be helpful for people with Syndrome X.

> My sister and I used to love to eat a snack to help us get to sleep at night when we were young: quick-cooking white rice with milk and sugar on it. I wouldn't eat such an unhealthy concoction now. However, I now know why we liked it.

CHEMICAL IMBALANCE

Sugar causes a huge chemical imbalance in your body that throws off the way your body works. It doesn't just happen. It comes from eating the wrong foods at the wrong times, not eating at all, or using caffeine and/or nicotine.

Sugar consumption is way up in North America. Researchers found that in the 1800s the average person in North America consumed about 12 pounds of sugar a year. In 2002 it was estimated that the average person ate about 150 pounds of sugar a year. If sugar is causing chemical imbalances that contribute to low blood sugar and Syndrome X, which then lead to anger, depression, violence, and fatigue, it is easy to see how violence and anger have increased in recent times.

How Muffins Have Changed

Muffins have been around for years, but how they've changed in the last twenty-five years! Until the late 1970s when chains of muffin stores opened in malls, muffins were more like biscuits. A batch of a dozen muffins that used $2\frac{1}{2}$ cups of flour had 2 tablespoons of sugar or honey. After what I call the muffin revolution, muffins with $2\frac{1}{2}$ cups of flour now contain at least a cup and a half of sugar; some even have 2 cups of sugar. A cup contains 16 tablespoons. That is a huge increase in sugar. Muffins were never supposed to be like a sweet roll or dessert. Muffins were more like biscuits. Muffins made with whole-wheat flour and bran were even considered health food in the 1960s and 1970s. Now all that is changed. And it isn't just muffins that have increased sugar. Everything has. As if that isn't enough, people are consuming more sugar every day in the form of soft drinks and candy. Is it any wonder that North Americans have chemical imbalances in their brains and bodies?

> We were walking from a meeting at about noon one day in the early 1980s, and one of the college women was drinking a can of caffeinated soft drink. She was talking about how her depression was a chemical imbalance. She said she felt so much better since she'd been taking a major antidepressant. When I asked her what she'd eaten for breakfast, she looked at me like I was a freak and replied she hadn't eaten breakfast—she never did. No surprise to me that she had a "chemical imbalance."

PREVENT HIGH BLOOD SUGAR AND INSULIN LEVELS

The ways to prevent high blood sugar and insulin levels are the same as the ways to avoid low blood sugar described in Chapter 2: Eat small, frequent meals; avoid sugar, refined flour products, fruit juice, dried fruits, bananas, caffeine, nicotine, processed foods, and stress. Eat every three to four hours, starting within a half hour of getting out of bed.

Now we'll add a few more: Never eat a big meal at one sitting. Eat low-glycemic carbohydrates if you eat carbohydrates. Make sure you eat at least five to eight servings of vegetables a day; several servings should be raw. If you make one meal a huge salad with a small amount of protein and a lot of fresh veggies, you will eat about half your daily quantity of veggies. Put veggies in everything you eat. Have veggies and protein for snacks. Make fresh veggie juice or take a green drink every day. Eat the foods, nutrients, and herbs that help keep your blood sugar from going drastically up or down. When you do this, you will be helping to prevent and overcome anger flare-ups in your life.

"After I got a really high score on the Syndrome X Test, I started taking the Anger Cure supplements you suggested. In three days my migraines were gone. In a week my fatigue was gone. The best results, however, were that my intense anger, negativity, and cravings started to go after only a few weeks. It's a slow process because I'm so addicted to carbohydrates that I find it difficult to give them up. But people at work are already noticing that I'm not flying off the handle at them as much or as quickly as I used to. The funny thing is that I didn't realize I was angry until it started to go. I'm sticking with this program."

Is There a Pill?

You can get many nutrients from your food or in supplement form that can help reduce symptoms of Syndrome X. Many supplements even have obvious names like SynX, Gluco-Balance, or GluControl. Just look in the health food store or ask your doctor. (Please make sure that the "glu" in the name is for glucose and not for glucosamine. They are not the same.) A lot of prescription drugs are also available now that will help, although herbs and minerals have been in use longer and are more helpful. The minerals magnesium, manganese, chromium, and vanadium are useful to help stabilize your blood sugar levels and prevent high insulin levels. Coenzyme Q_{10}, alpha-lipoic acid, folic acid, vitamins B_6, B_{12}, E, and C are also helpful. The herbs *Gymnema sylvestre,* bitter melon (*Momordica charantia*), fenugreek seed, ginkgo biloba, devil's club root (*Oplopanax horridum*), and hawthorn have all been used with great suc-cess in Asian medicine for centuries for blood sugar, insulin, or heart problems. Some of these are discussed below. A formula of sprouted seeds high in beta-sitosterol can improve immune function and help prevent or reverse many early prediabetes, type 2 diabetes, or Syndrome X symptoms. Super Sprouts Immune Enhancer contains fenugreek sprouts and other sprouts high in beta-sitosterol.

Magnesium

This mineral is a catalyst in helping carbohydrates become properly assimilated instead of being stored as fat. Magnesium helps the heart muscle in cases of myocardial infarction, hypertension, and congestive heart failure,[5] and it is useful in reducing high blood pressure. It also helps keep you calm. Magnesium can improve insulin response and action as well as how your body handles glucose. Magnesium is very important for people with insulin resistance and/or Syndrome X. The daily amount found to be useful is 400 milligrams (mg).

Manganese

Manganese regulates fat and carbohydrate metabolism. It is often useful in reversing tendonitis and is especially necessary for people with diabetes. About 10 mg a day is all you need.

Chromium

Chromium is very important for diabetes, insulin resistance, and Syndrome X because it helps break down sugar for conversion into energy and in the manufacture of certain fats. Chromium is often called the glucose tolerance factor (GTF) because it makes you more tolerant of sugar and carbohydrates. Glucose tolerance keeps sugar and carbohydrates from giving you mood swings. Chromium is a mineral that is essential for the health of your pancreas because it prevents your blood sugar from rising from a sugar load. Chromium increases the effectiveness of insulin, stimulates enzymes in the metabolism of energy, and promotes the synthesis of fatty acids, cholesterol, and protein. Chromium is found in whole grains and brewer's yeast. Most North Americans are deficient in chromium. A daily dose of 200 micrograms (mcg) is suggested.

Coenzyme Q_{10}

This relatively new nutrient is helpful for support of healthy blood cholesterol levels and can increase healthy HDL (high-density lipoprotein) levels, and stabilize blood pressure levels. Coenzyme Q_{10} plays a major role in creating energy in your cells and is also helpful for healing gum and heart problems. This antioxidant is generally taken in doses of 30 to 400 mg daily; the latter is useful in treating heart and gum disease.

Alpha-Lipoic Acid

Recent research has shown that daily doses of 600 mg of alpha-lipoic acid can reverse and prevent polyneuropathy in type 2 diabetics.[6] This antioxidant is very important for general health if you live in an area that has pollution of any kind, if you have ever eaten deep-fried foods or other rancid oils, or smoked tobacco products.

Vitamin E

This antioxidant has been used since the 1940s for heart disease, the health of arteries and mucus membranes, and relief of menopause symptoms. Many people feel it reduces aging of their skin, hair, blood vessels, and heart. Because it works so powerfully on your heart, it is best to start with a dose of 100 international units (IU) a day for several weeks and then increase it by another 100 IU for a few weeks until you get to the desired dose. A preventive dose is generally 400 IU a day, and for major heart disease men have been known to take up to 1,200 IU a day. (Please consult with your doctor before taking large doses of vitamin E.) It is best to use d-alpha-tocopherol as it is from a natural source. The label should read "mixed tocopherols" or include gamma-E. Mixed tocopherols include delta- and beta- along with alpha- and gamma-tocopherols. Any label that reads dl-alpha-tocopherol is synthetic vitamin E, which I don't recommend.

Gymnema sylvestre

This herb has been used in India for diabetes and blood sugar problems for centuries. It is used in Ayurvedic medicine. It can reduce the craving for sugar if taken as a supplement or, if a craving is bad, a capsule can be emptied directly onto your tongue to stop it.

Bitter melon (*Momordica charantia*)

This very wrinkled pale green gourd can be found in Chinese and East Indian grocery stores. It is also called karela. It is eaten in stews, soups, stir-fries, and other traditional dishes, but it is also used as a medicine for stabilizing blood sugar levels. It helps keep blood sugar levels from rising after meals and, therefore, keeps insulin levels lower. The juice was used in a study with diabetics, and it was found to significantly improve glucose tolerance.[7]

Fenugreek seeds

Fenugreek seeds, in teas or sprouted, have been used in European medicine to expel mucus from the digestive tract. More recently, research has shown that they improve glycemic control, decrease insulin resistance in type 2 diabetics, and can also lower triglycerides.[8] Fenugreek, also called methi, is the recognizable taste and smell of Indian curry.

Hawthorn

Hawthorn (*Crataegus*) has been used for hundreds of years in Europe, China, and Japan to support the heart and circulatory system.

ANGER, DEPRESSION, AND SUGAR

In the early 1970s I started doing nutrition counseling. Over the years I've seen people become more and more depressed and angry in about the same proportion as the increase in sugar in the daily diet and life of North Americans. That has now reached epidemic proportions. It is not the fault of the sugar companies or the food manufacturers. It is the fault of every person in North America who buys the sugar-laden products and consumes them. You are responsible for what happens to your body—for what you eat and what you don't eat. You have the choice. You can reverse anger and most of the other symptoms you have marked on the tests so far by taking charge of your diet and lifestyle. Make the decision today.

It you feel you can't help yourself when confronted with alcohol, sugar, or other carbohydrates, then you need to take some of the recommended nutrients and herbs as well as follow the recommended diet and eating patterns.

CHAPTER SUMMARY

1. Your lifestyle and emotional choices can harden your heart and increase the possibility that you will develop Syndrome X.

2. Anger is directly related to chemical imbalances in your body.

3. High insulin and low levels of many different nutrients can create the chemical imbalances that are part of Syndrome X and anger problems.

4. The glycemic index is a useful tool for locating which foods may be affecting you and how to choose the correct foods and food combinations.

5. Many herbs, vitamins, and minerals are useful in preventing Syndrome X and anger problems.

CHAPTER 6

Your Expanding Universe

We are constantly in a state of either expanding or contracting. Classical Asian philosophy describes this as yin (expanding) and yang (contracting). Scientists often talk of "our expanding universe." Can we expand too much?

Yeast makes bread dough rise when sugar is there to feed the yeast. This is good when you're making bread. But it is very bad when the yeast is in your body and is causing you to expand in an unhealthy way. Many health problems are caused by the action of yeast in your body. Since yeast lives on sugar, sweets and carbohydrates feed it. It even lives on fermented foods like cheese, soy sauce, wine, vinegar, and beer.

When I was a child, we used to make hard cider by taking fruit juice or apple cider and adding a slice of bread and some raisins. The action of the yeast in the bread on the sugar in the raisins and apple cider produced alcohol.

IS YOUR BODY A STILL?

If you have an overabundance of yeast in your body and you eat sugar, fruit, fruit juices, fermented foods like cheese, beer, wine, bread, soy sauce, vinegar, pickles, or even mold or fungi like mushrooms and tempeh, the yeast will make its by-product alcohol.

Katie said to me one day that she wakes up feeling achy, her head spinning, her muscles tense, and often sick to her stomach. Her back aches so badly she can hardly get out of bed. She described a perfect hangover! But she hadn't drunk alcohol. How could that be?

When Katie told me these symptoms in 1982, we hadn't heard much about yeast. The late Dr. William Crook didn't publish *The Yeast Connection* until 1983.[1] But then yeast problems became the newest health food syndrome. Yeasts, both good and bad, are rampant because of the lifestyle of most North Americans.

TAKE THE YEAST TEST

If you want to find out if you have a yeast problem, take the test on the following page.

WHAT YEAST DOES TO YOU

When you have one of the toxic types of yeast living in your body, it can cause a lot of seemingly strange health problems. The Yeast Test includes just a fraction of the many symptoms attributed to yeast problems. Did you know that yeast affects women more than men? Due to their menstrual cycle women's fluctuating hormonal levels negatively affect the immune system, allowing women to be more susceptible to all kinds of immune suppression problems, including yeast.

Yeast lives in your body and produces toxins that can make you ill. One of the toxins acts just like alcohol in your body and many people have even failed a Breathalyzer Test because of the alcohol their own body produced.

So like Katie above, you may have all the symptoms of being drunk without drinking alcohol. In addition to having an overabundance of yeast living and growing in her body, Katie had daily exposure to toxins from formaldehyde-cured flooring. So at the same time as she was craving the foods that fed the yeast and getting sick, the environmental toxins were making her sick and adding to the toxins the yeast was making from her food. She was really ill and spent a lot of time in bed.

Sadly enough, the flooring that was giving off the toxic chemicals was in her bedroom. So she couldn't get over her illness without treating the yeast problem with diet and supplements and improving her immune function by abstaining from those foods and beverages known to trigger yeast growth.

YEAST TEST

Part 1

Mark off everything listed here that you have experienced in the last five years. Give yourself 1 point for each mark.

_____ Tiredness or fatigue not associated with physical work

_____ Strong smells really bother me, especially from perfume, cigarettes, or cleaning materials

_____ Sore muscles, especially on waking up

_____ Runny nose, front or back

_____ Frequent or constant constipation and/or diarrhea

_____ Irritability, crankiness, or quick temper

_____ PMS, premenstrual tension, or endometriosis

_____ Low or loss of sex drive and/or feelings

_____ Bouts of memory or concentration problems

_____ Fungus infection, including of the toenails, fingernails, or gums

_____ Vagina or penis irritation, itching, burning, oozing

_____ Itching of nose, eyes, ears

_____ Depression, blues, melancholy

_____ Neuropathy, numbness of hands or feet

_____ Frequent or recurrent sore throats

_____ Headaches

_____ Muscle cramps, especially at night

_____ Frequent bloating of the stomach, burping, acid reflux, or indigestion

_____ Allergies to grains

_____ Nerve deafness and resultant loss of hearing

_____ I feel sick, but my doctor can't find any reason for it

_____ Tobacco smoke bothers me

_____ I eat something with sugar in it almost every day

_____ My health problems seem worse on damp, muggy, or polluted days

_____ Feelings of being unreal, or spacey

_____ Some foods make me feel high or groggy

_____ I want to eat bread, sweet rolls, or drink beer or wine every day

_____ Angry flare-ups for no reason

_____ One or two alcoholic drinks makes me really high or drunk

_____ **Total for Part 1**

Part 2

Mark off any of the following that have been in your life at any time. Give yourself 1 point for each mark.

_____ Moldy, damp, or mildewy environment inside or outside

_____ Moldy, damp, or mildewy basement, attic, or garage

_____ Frequent use of strong-smelling chemicals like cleaning fluids, dry-cleaning chemicals, bleach

_____ Frequent exposure to smoke, first- or secondhand

_____ Use of antibiotics

_____ Use of steroids for asthma or arthritis

_____ Birth control pills or pregnancy

_____ Toxic chemical exposure

_____ Stress

_____ Anger or hatred directed toward you

_____ Feeling of being unloved

_____ **Total for Part 2**

_____ **Grand Total (Parts 1 and 2)**

What's Your Score?

Did you score 0 to 5? If so, yeast may not be a problem for you, but it could be a problem if you also scored over 15 on the Low Blood Sugar Test in Chapter 2. Did you score 5 to 15? Yeast may not be a big problem for you, but it could be involved in other health problems. Did you score 15 to 20? If so, yeast is really a problem for you. Did you score 20 to 38? Then yeast is definitely a problem for you. So if you got any score over 5 on this test, you need to read this chapter. But, as always, if you had 5 or less, you probably don't need to read it. On the other hand, you might have a friend or family member for whom yeast is a problem, so read on anyway.

Yeast Expands

Small amounts of yeast are normal in your system. Too much is not good. Yeast expands when it comes in contact with things that make it grow. It can cause your body to expand and produce obesity. It can cause your mind to be spacey and airy, resulting in poor thinking and failing memory. It can cause your organs to expand and produce all kinds of health problems. The foods that trigger yeast growth also create a rise in blood sugar and insulin, and the yeast produces alcohol as a toxic byproduct, which also raises blood sugar and insulin levels. Excess insulin levels lead to increases in body fats (both cholesterol and triglycerides), high blood pressure, and weight retention.

Not a New Problem

Yeasts, molds, and fungi are all responsible for yeast problems that have been around since the beginning of time. The Bible even talks about this and gives a cure for too much yeast.[2] Yeast is on most fruits and vegetables and even in the air. Certain kinds of yeasts are beneficial. Many antibiotics are made from yeasts or mold. You have had contact with various kinds of yeast or mold all your life. It's only when yeasts get out of control and begin to grow or "work" that they cause problems. If you don't have any symptoms listed in the Yeast Test, then you don't have to worry about yeast being a problem.

Are Yeast Problems Contagious?

Yes and no. Every book I have read about yeast talks about passing the yeast problem between people during sexual activity. Any contact between two people that involves exchanging fluids orally or genitally can pass yeast to the other party. This includes intercourse, open-mouth kissing, and oral sex.[3] While a man can have a yeast problem and not have any symptoms, he can still pass it to his partner since women are more susceptible because of their menstrual cycles. If you are a male and have jock itch, you have a yeast problem for sure. If you have enlarged fingernail or toenail beds because of a fungus infection in your nails, then you are sure to pass the yeast problem on through sexual contact.

CANDIDA ALBICANS

The most common type of yeast that can adversely affect your health is called *Candida albicans*. There are others, but this is the main one. Many people react to the yeasts or molds that grow on leftovers, cantaloupe and other soft-skinned melons, and cheeses, especially those that actually use *Candida albicans* as the catalyst for aging like Camembert. Some people react to mushrooms, cheeses, soy sauce, bread, unleavened bread, and nuts and seeds, especially peanuts and cashews. Some people can eat fruit, and others can't. Some people can eat grains, and others can't. It is so individual that you have to be a detective to figure out what affects you and what doesn't. If your test score showed that yeast is a problem for you, then you won't want to eat any high yeast or fermented foods (see "Foods to Avoid" on page 105). Having a yeast problem is another reason not to have multiple sex partners, share clothes, especially underwear, or kiss somebody on the mouth.

Garlic, the Stinking Rose

The stinking rose is very helpful in reversing yeast problems. Yes, that's correct, garlic. Aged garlic extract has been used for twenty years to combat yeast problems. Many people don't want to eat raw garlic, and aged garlic extract is the next best thing. You can either take odorless garlic or a very tiny piece of raw garlic.

Herxheimer Reaction

"Kathleen, I'm pregnant, and it's all your fault." Margaret called me after she started on raw garlic and aged garlic extract supplements and a special diet to reduce her candida problem. Before I could even comment she said, "I've been pregnant before. I know how it feels. It must have been the garlic or the candida diet."

Since Margaret already had four children but a new husband, I knew the diet hadn't done anything to make her pregnant. She assumed she was pregnant because she had breast and ovarian tenderness and a swollen abdomen. But she took a pregnancy test, which turned out negative, and then went out of town to work. Margaret couldn't eat the raw garlic while she was traveling and in meetings all day, and her symptoms subsided. She wasn't really pregnant. She was having a Herxheimer reaction. That meant the garlic and the diet were killing off the yeast too fast, and the dead yeast and toxins were giving her worse symptoms than she had before. Generally known as "die-off," this can produce a violent reaction. For this reason, you need to go slow when treating a yeast problem. You won't know if your symptoms are from die-off or new symptoms from something else unrelated to killing the *Candida*. It's always best to start slowly when making any health changes. As always, tell your doctor what you are doing.

Beer and Pizza

Beer and pizza or burgers, fries, and soft drinks are deadly combinations that can make yeast grow in your body. Some holistic practitioners say that the first generation to take antibiotics who came of age in the 1960s is also the first generation to live on beer and pizza and the first generation to be ill from yeast-related problems. But they take it a step further and say that yeast has made a nation of people, starting with that generation, who, when they feel down, use drugs to feel high. You don't need to "get high" unless you are low. So if you or your children have trouble with drugs, you can be pretty sure that a nutritional problem is at the bottom of it. It could be yeast or just blood sugar since they go hand-in-hand, and the same foods trigger both problems. If every time you or someone you know gets angry after having a meal that triggers a yeast problem, you will want to follow the suggestions for reducing yeast problems.

If every time you or someone you know gets angry after having a meal that triggers a yeast problem, you will want to follow the suggestions for reducing yeast problems.

EXPANSION OR CONTRACTION

Yeast can cause you to expand. It fact it may cause endless expansion.

Too much expansion can be responsible for anxiety, pain, feeling spacey, allergies, depression, or digestive disturbances. In Asian medicine this is call a yin state. In North America we call a person in that state a space cadet or an airhead. A very long list of effects are related to yeast over-growth in your body. Only diet and supplements can rein them in.

There is an expression in Ayurvedic medicine: There is no pain with-out expansion or *vata*. *Vata* represents the characteristics of air, wind, expansion, dryness, and quick movements. Not all people classified as *vata* are people with a yeast problem, but all people with a yeast problem exhibit most of the characteristics of *vata*. Every little stress or stressor can also cause your body to contract. The fight-or-flight response includes contraction of your heart, arms, legs, back, chest muscles, digestive organs, and diaphragm, all in preparation for expanding through fight or flight. If each time you contract, you don't expand to balance it, you will soon shut down and harden up. This is especially true of your heart as well as your muscles.

Let It Go

Exercise, blowing off steam, anger fits, violence, and hitting are all ways of trying to release this contraction. Going without eating, using caf-feine or nicotine, eating huge meals, and eating mostly carbohydrates can all contribute to expanding and contracting. When your blood sugar goes up, you are expanding. When yeast grows in your body, you are expand-ing. When your blood sugar drops, you are contracting. You can become angry during any of these ups and downs.

Low Blood Sugar and Yeast

Low blood sugar and the cravings that result lead to yeast growth and set off a vicious cycle. Let me explain. When blood sugar in the body drops, most people reach for something to raise it. This is generally some-thing sweet, something with caffeine, both, or even nicotine. Although these substances raise blood sugar levels, they also trigger a yeast growth spurt. This gives you constant ups and downs all day. At the end of the day your body can be so exhausted you want more sugar, alcohol, caffeine, or nicotine just to keep going. The more you do this, the more damage you will cause to your body and mind.

Constant Contraction

If you have rage, anger, depression, or a quick temper, chances are great you are in constant contraction and expansion. Constant fight or flight. Constant highs and lows. People with type 2 diabetes often have anger or angry outbursts when their blood sugar is out of control. Funny how they are trying to release the contraction with something that on the surface seems to be an expansion, the angry outburst, but in reality is a contraction. That just puts the person deeper and deeper into contraction (shutting down and hardening) and produces the fight-or-flight response. Then when they eat sweets, alcohol, junk food, or carbohydrates, they cause an expansion as the yeast is triggered to ferment.

> *People with type 2 diabetes often have anger or angry outbursts when their blood sugar is out of control.*

Don had a really bad habit of drinking coffee all day and then eating a burger and fries from a fast-food restaurant around 3 P.M. every day. He was proud of it. Then one day he called me from the hospital. He'd had a heart attack, and the doctor said he also had diabetes. Syndrome X and yeast problems. Not a big surprise. He changed his lifestyle and now has none of the symptoms that sent him to the hospital.

Fibromyalgia Is Permanent Contraction

Fibromyalgia, a rheumatic disorder that affects soft tissues and causes muscle pain and stiffness, is a form of contraction that's been given a medical name. I consider fibromyalgia a constant case of contraction due to being stuck in fight or flight. Why not just call it what it really is: faulty lifestyle choices leading to blood sugar fluctuations, causing fight or flight and resulting in permanent contraction of the muscles, diaphragm, heart muscle, and stomach. When the stomach is contracted, it doesn't work very well and the very minerals needed to help your muscles relax—calcium and magnesium—can't be broken down in the stomach.

Things as simple as eating breakfast; staying away from caffeine, nicotine, and sweet foods such as fruits, sugar products, and carbohydrates; and eating every three hours can reverse fibromyalgia in a few days. Of course, you will also need to take calcium and magnesium, zinc, chromium, trace minerals, and a lot of other nutrients to fortify your body, but making the lifestyle changes will put you on the road to recovery. (See Chapter 8 for more information on the fight-or-flight response.)

Contraction Slows Digestion

"Don't bother coming to the dinner table if you are mad or having a fight with your sister. The food will just sit in your stomach anyway," my mother was fond of saying. Turns out she was right.

Acid reflux is another example of contraction leading to a condition that's been given a medical name. Each time you go into fight or flight you stop your digestion. How will you digest your food if you are contracted and shut down? You won't. So the food is stuck in the stomach for a prolonged period while the stomach tries to digest without full movement of the stomach muscles and without the digestive juices that were shut off during fight or flight. Because of the lack of absorption of nutrients, you don't have the proper amount of B vitamins necessary to regulate the valve opening to the stomach and it becomes lazy (flaccid). While your stomach is working very hard to digest, you might even have pain, but the food just sits there. Eventually, the valve starts allowing the gases from poor digestion and fermentation to back up into the esophagus, taking some of the partially digested fluid with it. That's what creates the sour backwash or sharp, bitter taste in your mouth or back of your throat. Sometimes it doesn't even get to your mouth; it just erodes the bottom of your esophagus. They have a name for that, too: Barrett's esophagus. Please see your doctor if you suspect Barrett's esophagus because it has been known to lead to cancer—all because of anger, poor lifestyle choices, and low digestive enzymes.

CONSTANT EXPANSION AND CONTRACTION =
CONSTANT FIGHT OR FLIGHT

For the most part, holistic practitioners consider acid reflux and heartburn to be problems of too little digestive acid, not too much. When you take an antacid, it helps for a very short time but in the long run causes the contraction of the stomach. This slows digestion even further, until you have a constant state of poor digestion, sometimes pain, and acid reflux or heartburn. When yeast is present in your system and you eat any of the foods it lives on, you will produce gas and experience poor digestion. Constant expansion and contraction = constant fight or flight.

Learning to Relax

Let's learn the natural art of relaxing or expanding to release contraction. This is the way you love yourself. Don't let every little thing cause your body to contract or shut down. Take charge of yourself and adjust your body chemistry so that you don't cause stress and have fight-or-flight reactions. Fear triggers the fight-or-flight response. Contraction is also caused by fear. Expansion releases fear and improves self-confidence. Control even the most infinitesimal cellular level of your body and you will be free—free of automatic reactions and automatic protection through contraction. You will no longer be caught up in letting things outside you (your environment) rule how you feel. You will be *pro*active instead of *re*active.

Reversing Contraction

Expanding by deep breathing and doing relaxation techniques can minimize contraction in a very short period of time as well as help prevent the fight-or-flight response. You might want to join a gym, use a treadmill, start a walking program, or practice yoga, tai chi, meditation, or Pilates to help release contraction and teach yourself to relax.

Digestive enzymes often release contraction with just one dose. Of course, you will have to take them with every meal until your digestion starts working effectively again. The nutrient-dense foods recommended in the Anger Cure program, supplements, exercise, proper chewing, and relaxation will bring back your youthfulness and improve your digestion.

YEAST CONNECTIONS

Yeast seems to be partly responsible for many health problems. Most of them come from a weakened immune system. Nobody is really sure if the yeast problem suppresses the immune system or if a suppressed or weakened immune system allows the yeast to cause health problems. Both could be true.

Smells, Immune Suppression, Yeast, and Anger

"When they first built the new laundromat in my neighborhood, I was fine when I went there to do my laundry. Then I moved away. Two years later I went back once. You wouldn't believe what happened," a student told me in class. "I stuck my head in the washing machine and it was moldy. I didn't think too much of it until I found myself yelling at the other patrons and even screaming at the owner."

Strong smells can also suppress the immune system. Every time you have contact with a strong smell you risk the possibility of suppressing your immune system. Deodorant, soaps, shampoos, laundry soaps and softeners (including dryer papers), perfume, cleaning fluids, cigarette and cigar smoke, mold, mildew, plastic wraps, plastic containers, synthetic fibers in clothing, window cleaners—anything that has a strong smell—can cause contraction and suppression of your immune system and allow yeast to expand in your body. This can lead to blood sugar problems, anger, rage, and even fatigue or insomnia. Please use unscented products on your body and in your home to help reduce the yeast/anger connection.

> *Anything that has a strong smell can cause contraction and suppression of your immune system and allow yeast to expand in your body. This can lead to blood sugar problems, anger, rage, and even fatigue or insomnia.*

Anger

Anger, depression, mood swings, aggression, and anxiety are all

Conditions Thought to Be Connected to Yeast Problems

Acne	Drowsiness	Memory loss
Alternating diarrhea and constipation	Eczema	Mood swings
	Excessive sweating	MS
Anal itching	Feeling spacey	Nail bed infections
Anger and/or aggression	Food allergies	PMS
Anxiety	Gas	Psoriasis
Autism	Gout	Rheumatoid arthritis
Bladder and/or vaginal infections	Hives	
	Hyperactivity	Thyroid or adrenal problems
Bloating	IBS	
Depression	Insomnia	Violent behavior[3]

related to yeast problems. They are also related to blood sugar and Syndrome X problems. It should be clear by now that you will have to work on all these problems to overcome your anger, no matter how small or large it seems. The good news is the diet for the Anger Cure addresses all these problems.

Foods

Many foods can contribute to yeast problems, and many can help overcome them. As we emphasized in Chapter 2, the most important meal of the day is breakfast, which should be eaten within a half hour of getting up. Avoid sugar and flour products like bread, pretzels, crackers, muffins, biscuits, pasta, and especially don't eat sandwiches. Some people can eat fruit or grains, while others find it impossible to do so and get over a yeast problem. Avoid caffeine and nicotine in any form; don't have caffeinated beverages; and don't breathe in secondhand smoke or take nicotine gum or patches. Stay away from starchy vegetables like potatoes, peas, corn, or lima beans.

Corn, the Killer Vegetable/Grain

"My first food was corn syrup in water and I have been trying to get over it ever since," said Susan, who had the worst health problems I'd ever seen. "I've become a universal reactor. I can't go near bread, beer, mold, fungi, mildew, smoke, strong smells like cleaning fluids, or laundry soaps or softeners. I have to live in my car to keep away from all the things that make me sick. I'm so allergic to things and people I hardly go anywhere. I'm sure it was the corn syrup that started this."

I really listened to Susan, who also had a lot of rage and anger problems that were directly related to her immune system's inability to function and keep her healthy. She told me that once in the street she smelled some really strong perfume and became so enraged that she actually tried to attack the woman wearing it but couldn't because of the crowd. I, too, was fed corn syrup in water as my first food and had a history of allergies, mucus problems, coughing, earaches, and other things that might not have occurred if I'd been given mother's milk.

The corn we have now is not the same as the food the early settlers to the Southwest found there. Modern science has done so much to make it a viable crop that now it's just starch and chemicals. No wonder corn causes such reactions in people. I personally don't believe we were meant to eat corn or feed it to our animals. I think that eating corn and/or corn-fed animals might be responsible for yeast, blood sugar, and immune system problems, including allergies. Corn is also hidden in so many processed foods that it's practically impossible to avoid.

I once did nutritional work with a woman who seemed healthy and physically fit. She closed the door to my office and in a stage whisper said, "I vomit. Can you help me?"

"Everybody vomits when they need to," I answered.

"No, you don't get it. I make myself vomit."

After looking at what she ate and when she made herself vomit, I said to her, "I think you are allergic to wheat and corn."

"How did you know? The best allergist in town told me that," she replied.

So I explained to her how the two substances cause swelling and made her want to relieve that by vomiting. On the days she did that, she lived on muffins from a local shop. The wheat flour and the cornstarch in the baking powder—and perhaps in the muffins themselves—were the culprits. Once she gave up the wheat and corn, she no longer needed to make herself vomit. She also said that she was no longer angry or yelling at her husband and children the way she had been. She may have had a yeast problem, but I suspected that wheat and corn allergies were really what made her want to vomit. Have a look at "Foods to Avoid"; to reduce yeast problems and help overcome anger and rage, steer clear of the foods in this list.

Foods to Avoid

Bacon	Dinner rolls	Pie
Bagels	Doughnuts	Pizza
Bananas	Fish sticks	Portabella mushrooms
Beer	Flour products	Potato chips
Bread	Fried chicken	Potatoes
Burgers with buns	Fruit juice	Pretzels
Cake	Grains	Processed cheeses
Candy	Gum, even unsweetened or artificially sweetened	Processed foods
Canned soups with MSG		Smoked fish
Cantaloupe	Ham	Smoked meats
Cheese, fermented and aged ones	High-fructose corn syrup	Soft drinks
		Soy sauce
Coffee	Hot dogs	Sugar
Coffee cake	Ice cream	Sushi
Cold breakfast cereals	Leftovers	Sweet rolls
Cookies	Luncheon meats	Tempeh
Corn	Macaroni and cheese	Tobacco
Corn and other chips	MSG, especially in Chinese food	Vinegar
Corn syrup		Wine
Crackers	Mushrooms	Yeast
Deep-fried foods	Peanut butter	All the high-glycemic foods listed in Chapter 5
	Peanuts	

REAL FOOD

That leaves only real food to eat. Fresh food. Food you make yourself. The main difference between the foods to be avoided for low blood sugar and Syndrome X and those to be avoided for yeast is that some of the same foods should be avoided for all three. In the case of yeast you also have to avoid everything that is fermented or aged because fermented or aged foods encourage yeast to grow. But then again so do fruit or grains, and they are high-glycemic foods. Though vinegar can reduce the glycemic index of a food or meal, it is a fermented food and should be avoided by anybody with a yeast problem. "Foods as Medicine for Yeast" lists some foods that reduce yeast problems and help overcome anger and rage.

Essential Foods for Healing Yeast Problems

Of all the foods that are essential for healing yeast problems the most important ones are natural unsweetened yogurt, garlic, flaxseeds and flaxseed oil, olive oil and olives, foods high in B vitamins like liver and chicken livers, pumpkin and sunflower seeds, walnuts, shiitake mushrooms, alfalfa and fenugreek sprouts, and parsley. Any foods that help to overcome yeast by either killing it, as garlic is reputed to do, or preventing it from living, like yogurt is reputed to do, are good to eat.

Any foods that are known to support a healthy immune system like olives and olive oil or shiitake or maitake mushrooms are great to eat.

Yogurt capsules have become very popular for improving gut health and preventing yeast from living in the gut. Yogurt is a probiotic/prebiotic, a healthy bacteria that restores the essential bacteria in your intestines, improves digestion, and changes the pH balance so that yeast cannot live. You might want to try the Health Alive brand Super Probiotic/Prebiotic Bacteria available from www.healthaliveproducts.com.

Any foods that are known to support a healthy immune system like olives and olive oil or shiitake or maitake mushrooms are great to eat. Pumpkin seeds are good because they contain zinc, a mineral known for building strength and health in your entire body and mind.

Foods as Medicine for Yeast

Arame
Asparagus
Avocado
Boston or bib lettuce
Brazil nuts
Broccoli
Brussels sprouts
Cabbage
Cauliflower
Chicken
Chicken liver
Clams
Cottage cheese
Cucumber
Dulse
Eggplant
Eggs
Endive, not bleached
Escarole
Fenugreek tea or sprouts
Fish
Flaxseeds and flaxseed
   oil

Green beans
Heart
Hijiki
Raw garlic (or odorless
   capsules if you just
   can't do garlic)
Kale
Kelp
Kohlrabi
Leaf lettuce
Lentils
Liver
Meat (most of the
   ones not listed in
   "Foods to Avoid")
Mustard greens
Natural, unsweetened
   yogurt
Nori
Octopus
Okra
Olive oil
Olives
Oysters

Parsley
Pistachio nuts
Pork
Pumpkin seeds
Red leaf lettuce
Red, green, or yellow
   peppers
Romaine lettuce
Shiitake mushrooms
Sprouted grain bread
   without yeast
Sprouts of all kinds
Squid
Summer squash
Sunflower seeds
Tofu
Tomatoes
Turnips
Turtle
Walnuts
Watercress
Zucchini

EFFECTIVE EXERCISE AND TREATMENT

Dr. John Diamond was instrumental in popularizing a simple exercise that could build up your immune system and help overcome all kinds of health problems. I first read about it in the late 1970s in his hardcover book, *BK: Behavioral Kinesiology.* In 1980 he published the same material in a paperback called *Your Body Doesn't Lie.* Warner Books published the latest edition in 1994. He explained, based on research, the kinds of things that could suppress your immune system and the kinds of actions that could help rebuild it. Looking down at the floor constantly or looking at people frowning can reduce immune function. Looking up or looking at people smiling can improve immune function. He showed using kinesiology (also known as muscle testing) that eating sugar or wearing synthetic clothing can drag down your immune system. What did he describe as the most useful action you could do to improve your immune function? The thymus thump.

The Thymus Thump

The thymus gland is in the very center of your breastbone in the middle of your chest. To do the thymus thump, tap lightly on the spot above the thymus gland and the thymus will start to secrete T-cells to build up your immunity. It is so important to remember to do this if you have a yeast problem. It can revitalize your thymus and improve your basic immunity. I have seen people who were coming down with a cold or the flu do this every ten minutes or so and short-circuit the illness. Anytime you feel your energy being drained from you, do the thymus thump. If you walk past strong-smelling chemicals and feel weak-kneed, tap your thymus. If you walk past mushrooms in the rain and feel your stomach or head begin to ache, tap your thymus. If you sit next to someone who is wearing moldy clothing and you feel dizzy, tap your thymus. You can use the tips of your fingers and tap lightly or you can use your knuckles and thump vigorously. Just remember Tarzan and how he thumped his thymus; he stayed healthy.

That probably seems like the silliest thing I've written so far. It even sounds that way to me as I write it. However, I have used this technique with people for over twenty years and doctors who are friends have used it with their patients, and it really works. It isn't going to rid you of candida overnight, but it will help you feel better. If someone sneezes on you in an elevator, thump your thymus and you won't get the cold—well, unless you are really, really rundown. Then you will probably get it no matter what you do. There may be times when you'll have to do it for a friend or loved one because they can't do it themselves. Go ahead. Why not try it right now on yourself?

Sprouts Can Build Your Immune System

Some sprouted seeds can build immunity and help your body reduce the yeast population. Beta-sitosterol and beta-sitosterolin are the main active ingredients that have been shown for more than seventy years to modulate the immune system. They can make both an underactive and overactive (autoimmune) system return to normal and, thus, help reduce immune system problems. Since yeast problems, diabetes, and Syndrome X are all signs of reduced immune function, it would behoove all of us to grow our own sprouts and eat them frequently. See my book *Sprouts: The Savory Source for Health and Vitality* (Alive Books, Vancouver, B.C., 2000) for sprouting instructions.

The sprouts highest in beta-sitosterols and beta-sitosterolins are amaranth, buckwheat, barley, fenugreek, sunflower, and flaxseed. Try sprouting them yourself or take the Health Alive brand supplement Super Sprouts Immune Enhancer available in stores or from www.healthalive products.com.

See Your Doctor

If you suspect that you have a major yeast problem, especially if you think it has been affecting your life for years, please ask your doctor to test you for it and take whatever antifungal medication he or she prescribes. You will still want to follow the eating plan outlined here. It can take anywhere from four weeks to up to two years to overcome the effects of a life-long yeast infection. You must work diligently to get rid of it. You can't cheat at all or the yeasts will just grow again. Yeasts secrete mycotoxins (poisons) that can cause all kinds of health problems, but they may also try to fool you into thinking you need sugar, yeast, or carbohydrates to maintain their status quo. It is very important to keep your bowels functioning so that you keep the dead yeasts moving out of your body and also get rid of the mycotoxins the yeasts have been giving off.

Water and Fiber

It is essential to drink eight to ten glasses of pure water a day and to consume fiber every day. High-fiber foods are useful in removing any putrefied material that might be lodged in your intestines, which is what yeasts live on. What foods are high in fiber? Romaine lettuce, green beans, parsley, sprouts, psyllium seeds, and most vegetables, especially sea vegetables like kelp, hijiki, wakame, and nori.

Exercise Daily

Working your body daily is a great way to work out anger, rage, and other toxins in your mind and body. If you want to feel really good, you'll want to exercise every day. Add exercise to your life by walking up stairs whenever you can. Walk to the store instead of driving. Park at the far end of the parking lot and walk to the store. Once you start doing more exercise, you'll feel better and want to do even more. Many times yeasts live in the sludge that stays in your body. Water, fiber, and exercise can help work that out.

SUCCESS IS YOURS

This focus on yeast has added only one new thing to the Anger Cure program: special foods to eat and to avoid. Everything else is the same: avoid caffeine, nicotine, sugar, flour, sweet fruits and fruit juices, carbohydrates without protein, and the foods in the avoid list that make yeast grow. Eat every three hours and eat breakfast within a half hour of getting up. Eat as many vegetables as you can every day; try new ones once in a while for variety. Take olive leaf extract, aged odorless garlic, sprouts high in sterols, and probiotics in pill form to really get rid of yeast.

CHAPTER SUMMARY

1. Yeasts live on all foods, and they also live in your body. Too much yeast living in your body can cause health problems.

2. Expansion and contraction related to yeast growth and other factors goes on in your body all the time.

3. Garlic and natural yogurt are useful in combating yeast overgrowth.

4. Antibiotics, molds, yeasts, and anger can suppress your immune system and encourage yeast growth that causes health problems.

5. Yeast overgrowth can lead to anger, rage, fatigue, depression, and a host of other health problems.

6. Exercising, practicing relaxation techniques, deep breathing, and avoiding sugar, carbohydrates, alcohol, tobacco, and caffeine can improve your health.

7. The thymus thump can help build up your immune system.

8. Sprouts contain beta-sitosterol and beta-sitosterolin, which help increase immunity and reduce yeast and blood sugar problems.

CHAPTER 7

How Your Body Creates Anger

"Sometimes I think my body is working against me," my friend Donna said one day. "Just when I think I'm strong enough to work all day and not get excited, cry, or come home so exhausted at night I can hardly make supper, something sets it off and I fall into the same pattern again."

Do you have days when you experience unexplained fatigue, anger, crying spells, nervousness, or poor concentration? Does it seem like your body is reacting inappropriately given what's actually happening?

TAKE THE GENERAL HEALTH TEST

Take this test to see how many body functions have become affected by your lifestyle.

BASIC UNIT OF ENERGY

As we discussed in Chapter 2, the body runs on a basic unit of energy called blood sugar that comes from food. Every part of your body uses blood sugar as the basic unit of energy. So every time you eat food, you get energy.

FOOD = ENERGY

NO FOOD = NO ENERGY

Many people have not grasped the simple concept that if you do

113

GENERAL HEALTH TEST

Mark all that apply to you now or in the last six months. Give yourself 1 point for each mark.

_____ Trouble waking up in the morning

_____ Insomnia or trouble falling asleep

_____ Bloating after meals

_____ Constant thirst

_____ Chew gum or eat candy daily

_____ Stay at home evenings and weekends

_____ Joints ache

_____ Poor circulation

_____ Bunions

_____ Ingrown toenails or spoon-shaped fingernails

_____ Wake up after a few hours sleep, hard to get back to sleep

_____ Asthma or other breathing problem

_____ Catch every cold or flu going around

_____ Feel weak after a cold or the flu

_____ Get hoarse or have laryngitis often

_____ Eyes and/or nose watery

_____ Irritable before meals

_____ Yawn mid-morning or mid-afternoon

_____ Feet smell

_____ Bitter or metallic taste in the mouth on awaking

_____ Headaches frequently

_____ Tire too easily

_____ Sensitive to hot weather

_____ Nightmares or bad dreams

_____ Coated tongue

_____ Highly emotional

_____ Ringing in the ears

_____ Constipation or diarrhea

_____ **Total Score**

What's Your Score?

The symptoms in the test indicate the ways your glands and organs, including your heart, liver, thyroid, stomach, adrenals, and immune system, can be out of balance. What was your total score? Did you get 28? I sure hope not! The correct answer is 3 or less, and even that might be too many for a healthy person. If you got 2 or less, you may not need to read this chapter, but I suggest you do anyway. Once you understand the way your body works (and most everybody else's as well), you will understand why some people are ill and others are not.

not eat, you won't have energy, so they go without eating during an average day.

Your Body—Your Car

If we compare your body to a car, you might see the bigger picture here. If you tried to run your car or truck without gas or oil, what would happen? It would break down. Some parts might even get so damaged they would have to be replaced. Well, it's the same with your body. The main difference between your car and your body is that your car will not run without gas. However, you can push your body to run without any fuel, and that gradually breaks it down and causes damage.

Your car would not work if you put soda pop in the gas tank. Your body will. Your car is very specific about the kinds of fluids it needs and how it functions once it gets them. Your body isn't as discriminating as your car; it will work even when you give it incorrect fuels. At least in the short run it will. But eventually it will just wear down and wear out.

More About Your Score

If you scored more than 4 or 5 on the General Health Test, you are wearing out your body. Unless you tell me you're over ninety years old, then you might expect some of the parts to be wearing out. A healthy person generally doesn't get more than one cold a year, if that. A healthy person can wake up first thing in the morning and be alert. A healthy person never has a bad taste in his or her mouth at any time of the day or night. A healthy person doesn't get mood swings, fatigue, backaches, or have ingrown toenails. A healthy person doesn't gasp for air when they run up a flight of stairs.

Blood Sugar Levels

Every time you eat food, your body turns it into blood sugar, which raises your blood sugar level and gives you energy. In order for your body to use the energy from the blood sugar, it secretes insulin to transform the blood sugar into energy. That's a pretty simple chemical process that only happens if you eat something. It generally takes about three to four hours in a healthy person for the blood sugar to be utilized, and then your blood sugar level goes down gradually, you begin to feel hungry, and then you know it's time to eat. Figure 7.1 shows what that looks like on a graph.

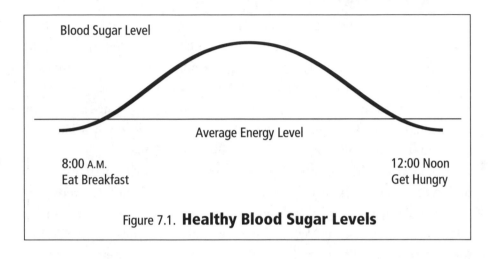

Figure 7.1. **Healthy Blood Sugar Levels**

FALSE ENERGY PRODUCERS

Some things you eat, use, or drink produce the same response as food, except that they are not really food. I call them false energy producers. They are nicotine and caffeine. Coffee and cigarettes can cause your blood sugar levels to go up, but only for a short time. They aren't food so they won't be in your stomach like food would be for a long period of time. Instead of your blood sugar levels going up and then gradually coming down over three or four hours the way they do with food, you get a rise in your blood sugar levels that lasts around one hour or less. Then you have to keep using nicotine and/or caffeine to keep pumping up your blood sugar levels to have the energy to function. That is what makes people think coffee and cigarettes are addictive. You have to have them every hour or so to keep bringing up your blood sugar levels. I call this false energy because it doesn't come from food and it doesn't last very long.

Smoking tobacco products and drinking caffeinated beverages daily is a good way to cause a breakdown in your body and wear it out fast. It's kind of like putting a half-cup of low-grade gasoline in your car and going on a trip. You have to stop every few minutes to get more, and eventually your engine will be so dirty it will not function properly. Each time you drink caffeine, smoke, or chew tobacco your blood sugar goes up and then falls further down than where it was when you started. So you have to keep smoking or drinking caffeine to get more energy, even though it's false energy. Figure 7.2 shows how that looks.

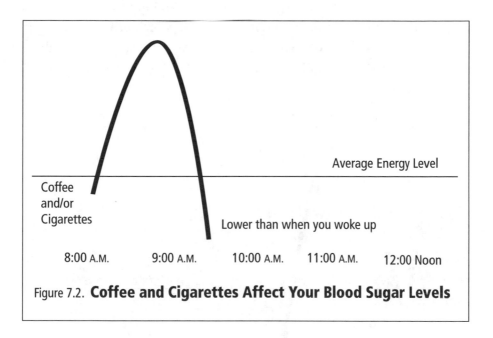

Figure 7.2. **Coffee and Cigarettes Affect Your Blood Sugar Levels**

We were taking a Kundalini yoga class and the teacher said, "According to our teachings you can't trust a person who smokes." There was a huge gasp in the room, mainly from the smokers. For nearly thirty years I have noticed that he was correct. Smokers are more likely to fly off the handle or have anger problems than nonsmokers. You never know when they might react with anger or violence.

Anger Levels

Because of the way your body reacts to these two nonfoods, it can make you feel angry a lot of the time or have angry reactions, mainly because your blood sugar levels are going up and down so often. Giving up caffeine and nicotine are two really good ways to reduce your anger levels.

False High

If you get up in the morning and eat something with sugar in it, you can give yourself a false high. Sugar and products made with sugar can raise your blood sugar levels higher than non-sweet foods. So your blood sugar goes up high, you secrete a lot of insulin, which uses up the blood sugar faster than the blood sugar from nonsugar food, and your blood sugar levels crash. That's why it's called low blood sugar. Figure 7.3 shows how that looks.

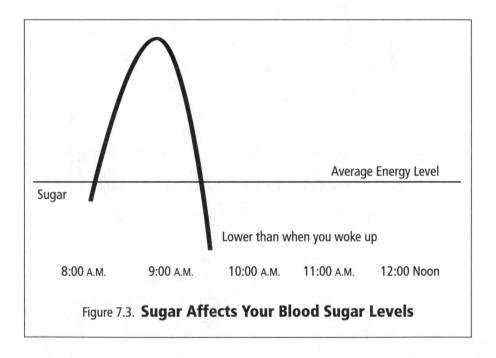

Figure 7.3. **Sugar Affects Your Blood Sugar Levels**

Often the sugar high causes a rebound so your energy level drops below where it was before you ate the sugar. If you have coffee with sugar and a cigarette, you will get about the same result. Figure 7.4 shows how that looks.

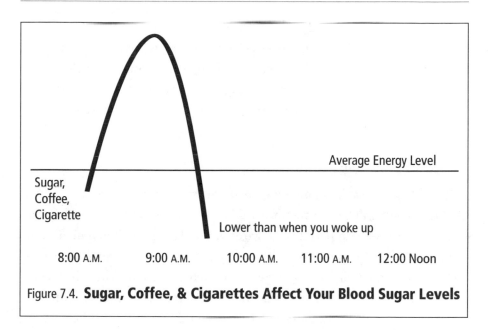

Average Energy Level

Sugar,
Coffee,
Cigarette

Lower than when you woke up

8:00 A.M.   9:00 A.M.   10:00 A.M.   11:00 A.M.   12:00 Noon

Figure 7.4. **Sugar, Coffee, & Cigarettes Affect Your Blood Sugar Levels**

Avoid the Highs and Lows

You can avoid frequent highs and lows by eating breakfast and the low glycemic foods discussed in Chapter 5 and by taking some of the suggested herbs and minerals. That will keep your blood sugar levels about the same throughout the day, especially if there is a small amount of fat in the meals. Figure 7.5 shows how that looks.

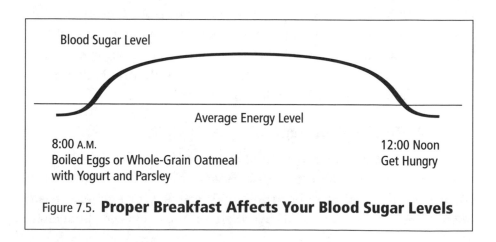

Blood Sugar Level

Average Energy Level

8:00 A.M.   12:00 Noon
Boiled Eggs or Whole-Grain Oatmeal   Get Hungry
with Yogurt and Parsley

Figure 7.5. **Proper Breakfast Affects Your Blood Sugar Levels**

There are no real highs or real lows. You have constantly available energy to use for thinking, working, feeling, or just living. You will be happy and healthy. You will not have fatigue, depression, low self-esteem, or anger. You will look and feel young and vibrant. You will not need stress or anger-management classes. When your blood sugar energy is used up, you will naturally feel hungry and eat something.

Addiction Begins Innocently

Addiction to caffeine, nicotine, or sugar can begin innocently enough. One day you don't have time for breakfast so you just grab a cup of coffee, something sweet, and perhaps a cigarette. You feel great. Then in an hour or so you start to come down. You feel yucky. Your nose runs, your eyes are blurry, your hands shake, your stomach is queasy, and your body starts to ache, feel tired, or worn down. So you reach for another coffee or sweet. After all, it's right there in front of you all the time. While you are having the coffee you might as well have a cigarette, so you go outside and drink coffee and have a cigarette. Right away you feel good again. Somewhere deep inside your mind the link between being down and having a coffee or cigarette is embedded along with feeling better afterward.

In a study conducted in the United Kingdom, women who were going through withdrawal from caffeine in coffee or tea were given diet soft drinks either with caffeine or without. The group that drank the caffeine felt improvement in their mood and feelings of pleasure along with a rise in their systolic blood pressure. Of course, the biggest problem with this study was that the researchers also gave the women a brand-name chocolate bar before the study results were measured. Since sugar can affect mood changes similar to those of caffeine, this wasn't wise. Furthermore, chocolate contains substances similar to caffeine.[1]

Can't Face the Morning?

When you wake up in the morning and you can't face the day, you could have several different medical and/or metabolic problems. You could have an underactive or hypothyroid gland. Your immune system might be suppressed. You could have allergies. You might even be anemic.

You could be getting too little or not deep enough sleep. Your doctor can check out all these possibilities. However, the main reason most people can't wake up in the morning or face the day is faulty lifestyle and low blood sugar.

Every part of your body needs blood sugar to function. If your brain has none, it won't work, and you won't be able to function properly. You might describe it as being foggy or feeling like you were run over by a truck during the night. You might even think that you didn't sleep well. That is often the case. You need to have stable blood sugar levels to be able to sleep through the night. If you don't, every time your blood sugar drops, it wakes you up, either com-pletely or partially. If you wake up fully, you may think you woke up to urinate and walk to the bathroom. The walking raises your blood sugar, and you fall back to sleep. If you wake up only slightly, you just toss and turn throughout the night, so that you never really get deep relaxing, regenerating sleep. When you wake up feeling tired, it generally signals that your blood sugar has dropped drastically during the night. You might be committing one of the lifestyle errors dis-cussed below.

You need to have stable blood sugar levels to be able to sleep through the night. If you don't, every time your blood sugar drops, you will wake up.

LIFESTYLE ERRORS

A client once kept a record of her habits for me. The last thing she and her husband did at night was smoke a cigarette. The first thing they did in the morning was smoke a cigarette. Then once they got going a little they had coffee and another cigarette. This continued until she ate something about five hours later. Usually it was a cookie or lemon square. She had dozens of things wrong with her (health problems and symptoms her doctor called dis-eases) that could easily be fixed by the proper lifestyle.

Many people have no idea how their lifestyle choices affect their health. Let's take a look at four common errors.

Error 1

The most common error is eating a big meal at night or eating late at night. That makes your blood sugar go up really high before you go to bed. You secrete insulin to use up the blood sugar. But because your blood sugar is so high you secrete a lot of insulin, and it makes your blood sugar fall further down than it should during the night. So when you wake up in the morning, your brain doesn't have the blood sugar it needs to function and you can't think clearly. This wastes a lot of time in the morning. Coffee, cigarettes, and sugar can rescue you by bringing up your blood sugar quickly so you can function. This is a trap! As soon as you have the first coffee, cigarette, or dose of sugar, you start down the slippery slope of becoming addicted to them. You become addicted to what these chemicals do to your blood sugar. Eating real food would serve you better and stop the addiction; even veggie juice would work better. Figure 7.6 illustrates how addiction starts.

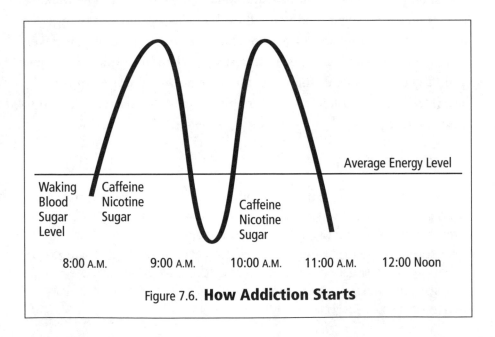

Figure 7.6. **How Addiction Starts**

To perk yourself up in the morning you start the up and down of drug addiction. This can also be a reason you wake up very low in the morning.

If you are up and down all day like the example in Figure 7.6, that can cause your blood sugar to go lower than it should at night.

Error 2

You go without eating for more than four hours. Think about how your body works. Remember food = energy, and no food = no energy. If you don't eat, your blood sugar will drop and set you up for confusion, anger, poor concentration, as well as all the things you marked off on the Low Blood Sugar Test in Chapter 2 and all the symptoms you marked off in the Syndrome X Test in Chapter 5. Anger is in both of them. Figure 7.7 shows what no food = no energy looks like.

				Average Energy Level
No Food or Caffeine or Nicotine or Sugar	Groggy Foggy Angry			Can't Think
8:00 A.M.	9:00 A.M.	10:00 A.M.	11:00 A.M.	12:00 Noon

Figure 7.7. **No Food = No Energy**

Error 3

You eat breakfast but don't eat another meal until dinner. That means you have raised your blood sugar with some food, then to keep it up so you can function you have gum, coffee, doughnuts, candy, soft drinks, or even a cigarette. Figure 7.8 on the following page shows how that looks.

Error 4

You don't eat food or use caffeine, nicotine, or sugar all day long. By the evening you are so confused, angry, exhausted, or fatigued that you crave something–anything–to raise your energy level so you have a glass of wine or beer. Then you don't care if you eat anything.

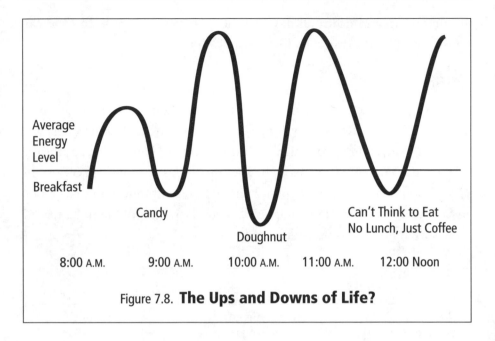

Figure 7.8. **The Ups and Downs of Life?**

HOW CAFFEINE AND NICOTINE TRIGGER STRESS

Caffeine and nicotine trigger the stress response in your body. In fact, any real or imagined stress, shock, or fear can trigger the fight-or-flight response. (Chapter 8 discusses the fight-or-flight response in detail.) Your body mobilizes to help you either get away from the stress or fight it. If you were being attacked by a wild animal or being mugged, this would be very useful to you. If all you had was a cigarette or a cup of coffee, it's harmful to you to go into fight or flight.

Not Enough Oxygen

Since oxygen is required by your muscles to relax and you are shallow breathing when you are in fight or flight, you won't be getting enough oxygen and you won't be able to relax. (Calcium and magnesium are also essential for relaxation.) During fight or flight your digestion is shut down, so you won't be able to get a supply of the nutrients you need to relax. Therefore, you will be tense and easily triggered into fear, anger, depression, or violence. Perhaps the slightest thing will set you off. You have to take some action to release the adrenaline roaring through your system and remove the tension from your muscles. What do you do? Yell at the kids? Hit the wall? Yell at other drivers? Go for a run? Threaten someone? Play a rough game of basketball? Work out at the gym?

Getting More Oxygen

A study done in the late 1960s in Sweden showed that more than 60 percent of smokers do so to get more oxygen. How is that possible? When you are shallow breathing, you are getting less oxygen. Drawing on the resistance of the cigarette forces you to use your diaphragm and you get more oxygen along with more smoke. You also release the shallow breathing. Think about how a smoker takes the first drag off a cigarette; that's deep breathing. Doing the deep breathing recommended in Chapter 3 can be a good start to reversing fight-or-flight tension and decreasing your desire for smoking.

Adrenaline Kicks In

When you go without eating, you create stress by trying to think or do anything requiring energy. Your body compensates for the lack of energy from food by going into the emergency mode of fight or flight. This chem-

---

Fight-or-Flight Reaction

Here is what happens in your body when you have a fight-or-flight reaction:

- Signal of stress or fear
- Breathing becomes shallow
- Adrenal glands respond
- Pupils dilate
- Adrenaline is pumped out
- Muscles tense up
- Heart rate goes up
- Digestion slows down or stops
- Glycogen (blood sugar) is released from the liver for emergency energy

All this is to prepare you to beat somebody up or run for your life—both physical actions. If you do not do something physical, you will stay in this state of hyperalertness. Every little stressor will trigger an angry reaction from you for the rest of the day.

ical reaction in your body was meant to save your life–and still could in times of need. Stress triggers the release of the hormone adrenaline that tells your liver to release blood sugar, your blood sugar comes up, and you are more or less fine until your blood sugar drops again in an hour. Figure 7.9 shows how that looks.

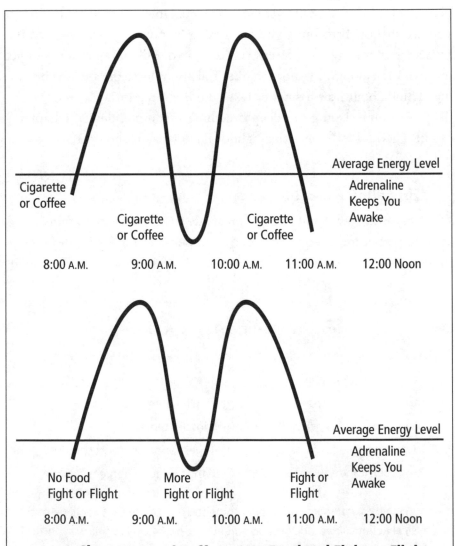

Figure 7.9. **Cigarettes and Coffee or No Food and Fight or Flight— It's All the Same**

Insomnia

Bethany used to say she was a night person. I always answered, "There is no such thing." I knew she had hypoglycemia and Syndrome X because I had given her the tests, and I also could see it in the way she craved sugar, carbohydrates, and caffeine and how quickly she got angry. She went on the Anger Cure supplements and lifestyle and began to live a normal life. Once her blood sugar was under control, she was no longer a night person.

When you have trouble getting to sleep or staying asleep because of adrenaline—your heart might be pounding, or you are fearful or worried—it's obvious that you have spent part or all of the day in fight or flight. This can come from caffeine, nicotine, sugar, or going without eating.

How Does Sugar Fit In?

When you use sugar to bring up your blood sugar level, it can cause your sugar level to drop quickly after only an hour or less. When this happens, your body can easily go into fight or flight to rescue your blood sugar levels and prevent stress. So you will either have to keep taking in sugar every hour or you will find yourself reaching for caffeine or nicotine. If you do none of them, your body will go into fight or flight on its own and create the same reaction of raising your blood sugar.

Sugar Water Starts It

Most babies are given sugar water in the hospital. Even those who will be breast-fed are often given a small bottle of sugar water. Doctors claim it's to make the bowels work. But breast milk is designed to be all that a baby needs. Until the late 1970s all baby food and formula contained both sugar and salt. It wasn't for the baby; it was for the mothers who tasted the food before giving it to the baby. I'm happy to say this practice has been stopped due to the campaigns of mothers and consumer-health activists. Now if we could just get the sugar out of cereals, breads, crackers, and all the other foods we eat, we could stop anger in our country. And we could stop nicotine and caffeine addictions as well. Our health costs would go down. There might be no need for old-age homes or nursing homes. We might even reduce the criminal population.

IT'S NOT YOUR FAULT

It's not your fault if you are addicted to nicotine, caffeine, or sugar. You can blame the sugar water, your baby food, the breakfast cereal, your teachers who gave you candy as a reward, your grandmother—the list might be endless. What is your responsibility is to leave all the blame behind and do something for yourself. Take charge of your life. Start by eating breakfast, without sugar or caffeine, of course. Then have small snacks of low-glycemic foods. Eat lots of vegetables every day. Exercise and take the nutrients you need for your own health.

CHAPTER SUMMARY

1. Food provides the basic unit of energy, blood sugar, that runs your body.

2. Caffeine, nicotine, sugar, white flour, and other carbohydrates can throw your blood sugar off, causing anger, rage, violence, depression, and low self-esteem.

3. Instead of eating the correct foods at the correct times, you can become addicted to caffeine, nicotine, and sugar to elevate your blood sugar levels.

4. Going without eating can cause the fight-or-flight response just the same as taking caffeine, nicotine, and sugar can.

CHAPTER 8

Anger and the
Fight-or-Flight Response

Delores and I were on the expressway going to her house in the suburbs.
She was driving. We were talking, and suddenly out of nowhere, Delores
was yelling and gunning the engine, "That blankety-blank, he cut me off."
The next thing I knew we were chasing him at extreme speeds,
weaving in and out of traffic.
"Delores," I said calmly, "what are you doing?"
She looked at me with fire in her eyes and said, "He cut me off and
he's going to pay!" And we were off again chasing him. I was finally able
to calm her down and stop this craziness, but it took its toll on her health.
Her anger and rage levels were as high as her stress levels, and she ended
up in bed with exhausted adrenals and chronic fatigue for several months.

Fight or flight is how your body reacts to some assumed stressor. It is a complex reaction that can, if continued over time, have harmful effects on all your glands and organs. Fight or flight can make you more high-strung, angry, and flighty. It can also damage your heart muscles, increase triglyceride and cholesterol levels, and do a lot of other damage to your body, which we will go into in this chapter. If you scored high on any of the tests so far, you will really want to read this chapter.

TAKE THE ROAD RAGE TEST

Take the Road Rage Test and see how you come out.

ROAD RAGE TEST

Mark off all that apply to you, taking the last year into account. Give yourself 1 point for each mark.

_____ Cut off another car in anger

_____ Yelled at a driver, pedestrian, or cyclist

_____ Mentally condemn drivers or the road system

_____ Made gestures to drivers in anger

_____ Chased a car in anger

_____ Bumped another car in anger in the parking lot or at a stop

_____ Made a sudden maneuver that is threatening, on purpose

_____ Imagined doing violence to another driver, pedestrian, or cyclist

_____ Repeated the story of how you "showed him" to other people

_____ Think you can "teach him a lesson" when other drivers don't act the way you want them to

_____ Got out of the car to yell at someone

_____ Tried to run another car off the road

_____ Actually got into a physical fight about driving

_____ Tried to run over a pedestrian or cyclist

_____ Carry a weapon in your vehicle

_____ Wrote down a license number with the intention of finding the person who cut you off

_____ Used your weapon against another driver

_____ **Total Score**

What's Your Score?

What did you score on the Road Rage Test? Is road rage one of the ways you exhibit the fight-or-flight syndrome? There is no good score for this test. If you marked off more than three, depending on which ones they are, you need help with road rage. Even three is three too many. Please read this book and follow the diet. You may also need anger-management counseling as well as the Anger Cure program if you got a score of 10 or more.

ANCIENT PROTECTION

The fight-or-flight syndrome or reaction is something left over from more primitive times. When the early settlers in North America were first crossing the country, they came across all sorts of situations that required them to fight or take flight to save their lives. Wild animals, sudden snow squalls, floods, trees falling, quicksand, Native people who didn't like strangers trespassing on their land, bands of robbers–the list is endless. These are not situations that most people face in everyday life today. Why, then, does your body still use this ancient protection mechanism?

Fight or flight is how your body reacts to some assumed stressor.

Let me repeat the definition of fight or flight: Fight or flight is how your body reacts to some assumed stressor. The key word here is "assumed." People who experience constant stress and exhibit fear, anger, depression, and a host of other symptoms listed in the Road Rage Test and in the tests in previous chapters are acting just like the pioneers did 150 years ago. It's a cellular response that responds to a faulty lifestyle. Of course, you might still need to use the fight-or-flight response in real-danger situations like a vehicle out of control in front of you on the highway or your child about to run into the street.

STRESS RESPONSE

A lot of different gland and organ systems are involved in the stress response. The pituitary gland, the adrenal glands, the heart, the brain, and the liver are all involved, but it is the adrenal response that is the most crucial for the stress response. The adrenal glands secrete the adrenaline that prompts the fight-or-flight response. If your adrenal glands are not healthy, you will have a lot of stress reactions when you don't want them.

"My Mom seems to be getting worse." Ronnie was really worried about his mother, and he had reason to be. "She flies off the handle all the time at the simplest things. A lot of the time she seems depressed. Then she yells at one of us kids and she seems better. I'm really worried for her. She has been smoking since she was in grade school; that's more than forty years. People are afraid of her because they never know how she will react to any situation. I don't even want to go to her house for dinner because there's generally a fight or screaming match. She never eats breakfast, just coffee and more cig-arettes. Do you think the stress of all that coffee and smoking have anything to do with the way she acts?"

Your Body: Both Smart and Stupid

Your body registers a stress and reacts. That's smart. Unfortunately, your body can't tell the difference between a siren on TV, one in your neighborhood, or one behind you on the road. That's stupid. If every time you hear a siren, no matter where it is, you react with a stress response, you can be sure that your stress warning system is out of balance. If your knees shake and your legs get weak when you drive by an accident that happened an hour before, your body is out of balance. Now, if the same thing happens when you're in an accident, it's not as stupid. That's a fight-of-flight reaction trying to get you to take some action to save yourself. That could be smart or stupid depending on the circumstances.

TAKE THE ADRENAL FUNCTION TEST

Take the Adrenal Function Test on page 133 and see if your adrenals are out of balance.

KNEE-JERK OR HAIR-TRIGGER RESPONSE

When your adrenal glands are exhausted because you have been using them to raise and lower your blood sugar almost daily instead of just in emergencies, you will notice that you fly off the handle or react quickly or violently to simple things. I call this knee-jerk or hair-trigger response. (A hair trigger refers to a gun. It only takes a hair to pull the trigger to shoot the gun. That isn't much.) That's how quickly it happens when a stressor is encountered or fear is aroused. That might have been fine 150 years ago when you were crossing the country in a wagon train or when you were out in the woods with wild animals all around. Well, no, even then it isn't good to have that kind of reaction. Almost everyone has seen someone react like that to a stimulus. You say something simple to some-one—something not meant to be offensive. The other person takes excep-

ADRENAL FUNCTION TEST

Mark off all that apply to you now or in the last six months. Give yourself 1 point for each mark.

_____ Chronic fatigue

_____ Fatigue from very little exertion or stress

_____ Low blood pressure

_____ Depression

_____ Angry or irritable, frequently

_____ Crave salty foods

_____ Poor circulation

_____ Bowel problems including diarrhea and/or constipation

_____ Skin has bronzing or looks tan without being in the sun

_____ Age or "liver spots" especially on face, hands, or arms

_____ Mood swings

_____ Finger and toenails have ridges or are weak

_____ Body hair seems to be decreasing

_____ Changes in weather bring on symptoms

_____ Respiratory disorders, especially asthma

_____ Allergies or hives, frequently

_____ White spots on fingernails

_____ **Total Score**

What's Your Score?

Did you get 16 or 17? If so, your adrenal glands are shot, and the Anger Cure diet and lifestyle plan will really help you. Anything more than 2 or 3 shows some level of adrenal exhaustion. Actually, you shouldn't have any symptoms marked if you are really healthy. However, anyone living or working in a modern city will have some of these symptoms. If you scored more than 3 or 4, you are having problems with stress because your adrenal glands are out of balance. There is hope for you. You will be able to recover and have no more reactions. A score of more than 4 may mean your adrenal glands are causing you to have angry reactions, lash out at people, or even smash things when you are angry, upset, or under stress.

tion to it, and–bang!–they react with an angry response. The slightest thing sets them off. This is a knee-jerk response.

Here are some different reactions to a stressful scenario: You are sitting in an open-air café and a car comes screeching to a halt and hits a tree near you.

Reaction 1: You jump and start screaming, but don't move. Your heart is pounding, your knees are shaking, and you can't do anything but scream. You could have been dead. This is not a good reaction.

Reaction 2: You look, see it, your mouth drops open, your eyes glass over, your heart rate speeds up, you watch it happen, but you can't react at all. You are just paralyzed. You could have been dead. This is not a good reaction.

Reaction 3: You jump up and start screaming and running around the table hitting your friends and saying things like, "Move, there is an accident here" or "Oh, my Gawd, you'll all be killed." You could have been dead. This is not a good reaction.

Reaction 4: You hear the tires start to screech a block away. You look around, get up, and move out of the way, motioning to your friends to do the same thing. This is a good reaction. You are not in danger because you have removed yourself from it.

What If Your Adrenals Are Exhausted?

Reactions 1 through 3 are the kinds of reactions a person with exhausted adrenal glands might make. Reaction 4 is the reaction of a person with healthy adrenal glands. In the first three reactions the person's adrenals secreted so much adrenaline that the person couldn't even think coherently enough to have a life-saving reaction. In reaction 4 the person had just the right amount of adrenaline to deal appropriately with the situation at hand. No knee-jerk or hair-trigger reaction.

If your score on the Adrenal Function Test indicates that your adrenals are overworked or exhausted, you will need to make some changes in your diet and sleeping habits to overcome that. You may even need to find a holistic doctor who can assess your situation and prescribe supplements and injections that will build up your adrenal glands. Following the suggestions in the Anger Cure is a good start, but you may require professional help. You're the best one to judge that.

ANGER AND YOUR ADRENALS

When your adrenals are exhausted or overworked, you may exhibit a lot of angry reactions. You may have a temper tantrum, as it used to be called. You might even hit someone and a few minutes later be really sorry. A person who beats up (physically or emotionally) on a wife or a husband is almost certain to have exhausted adrenals.

They Aren't Made of Steel

Your adrenal glands are delicate glands in the small of your back, just above the kidneys. They are intimately involved in blood sugar and insulin secretion, Syndrome X, diabetes, anger, stress, and fight-or-flight reactions. Every time you take caffeine, nicotine, sugar, or go without eating you are taxing your adrenal glands. Eventually, they will become so worn down that even the smallest stress your body and mind observe will cause a knee-jerk or hair-trigger reaction. When the adrenal glands are exhausted, they cannot discriminate; they just react to every little stress, real or imagined.

Horror Films and Scary Things

Every time you see a horror film, go to a scary movie, watch a murder in a movie, or see a car chase, you are exhausting your adrenal glands. Every time you do extreme sports like extreme skiing or extreme off-road mountain biking or run to catch a bus, you are calling on your adrenals to go into action. Every time you watch football, soccer, or basketball on TV, you are stimulating your adrenals to overfunction, which weakens them.

Violence and Children

A recent study of 119 inner-city seven-year-old students assessed the effect violence had on them. In this group 75 percent had heard gunshots, 60 percent had seen drug deals, 18 percent had seen a dead body outside, and 10 percent had seen a shooting or stabbing in the home. The tests were administered by a masked interviewer as part of the Culture-Free Self-Esteem Inventory. The conclusions of the test were that young inner-city children have a high exposure to violence by the age of seven and that this high exposure to violence correlates with poorer performance in school, symptoms of anxiety and depression, and lower self-esteem.[1] Unfortunately, researchers were not looking for a relationship between the violence the children experienced and their expression of violence and anger.

Real-Life Violence on TV

Let's look at two studies that consider the effects of separate incidents of violence or terrorism in the United States in recent times. In the first study conducted in the aftermath of the Oklahoma City bombing, results showed that children all over the country who watched the violence on television exhibited post-traumatic stress symptoms seven weeks after the incident.[2] The second study was done within three to five days after the September 11, 2001, terrorist attacks. It found that 44 percent of the adults surveyed reported one or more substantial stress symptoms from watching the event on television, while 91 percent had one or more stress symptoms.[3]

> "I went to my friend's house for the holidays and was shocked to see her eight-year-old son sitting in front of the TV playing some sort of video game," Aaron related to me one day over lunch. "He was yelling at the screen, jumping up and down, and hammering his fist into the couch. He was very angry and agitated and looked like he was in a trance. He was yelling, 'Kill, kill, I'll kill you.' When his mother called him to come to dinner, he lashed out at her in a way that was so violent, I couldn't believe it. My friend was proud of the fact that she didn't let her children watch TV, but I think the video games were worse for this little boy."

Television Viewing and Aggressive Behavior

A seventeen-year study of more than 700 families found that fourteen-year-old boys who watched three or more hours of television a day were about twice as likely as those who watched one hour a day to assault someone or get into a serious fight by early adulthood. Even after researchers adjusted for previous aggressive behavior, childhood neglect, family income, neighborhood violence, parental education, and psychiatric disorders, the results remained the same: There is a relationship between exposure to violence from video games, violent behavior and television violence in childhood, and violent actions later in life.[4]

TAKE THE LIVER FUNCTION TEST

Take the Liver Function Test to see if your liver is out of balance.

LIVER FUNCTION TEST

Mark off all that apply to you now or in the last six months. Give yourself 1 point for each mark.

_____ Sneezing attacks, especially in the morning

_____ Metallic taste in the mouth in the morning

_____ Pain in the back between the shoulder blades

_____ Pain or tenderness in the right side near the waist

_____ Bloated or full feeling

_____ Fatty foods cause distress

_____ Itching or burning anus

_____ Distress from dairy products

_____ Halitosis (bad breath)

_____ Dry skin

_____ Feelings of restlessness, anger, or agitation

_____ Skin peels on soles of feet

_____ Hair falls out in excessive amounts

_____ Queasy-type headache, especially over the eyes

_____ Skin itches, worse at night

_____ Skin and/or the whites of eyes look yellow

_____ Light-colored stools

_____ **Total Score**

What's Your Score?

Did you get 16 or 17? If so, your liver is in distress. Anything more than 2 or 3 shows some level of liver exhaustion. Actually, you shouldn't have any marked off if you are really healthy. However, anyone living or working in a modern city will have some of these symptoms. If you scored more than 3 or 4 on the test, you're having problems with stress because your liver is out of balance. But there is hope for you because the liver can repair itself in many cases. If you have been a serious smoker, alcohol imbiber, or coffee drinker, you may need a lot of help.

A score of more than 4 may mean your liver is causing you to have angry reactions, lash out at people, or even smash things when you get angry or are upset or under stress. The opposite is also true; anger reactions, lashing out at people, and smashing things may have caused part of your liver problem in the first place. If you scored more than 5 or 6, please see your doctor. You may have a serious, as yet undiagnosed problem that can be helped if you treat it early.

YOUR LIVER HAS A ROLE IN ANGER, TOO

In traditional Chinese medicine (TCM) every organ has an emotion associated with it. According to TCM, the liver is the seat of anger. That means if your liver is overworked, you will have anger, and if you have anger, you will trigger liver imbalances. That may or may not sound preposterous, but it is also something that holds true in Western medicine as well. Every time your blood sugar drops and you don't do anything about it, the stress signals the fight-or-flight response. The end result of this adrenal cascade is that your liver releases glycogen or blood sugar to raise your blood sugar levels so that you can function. Every time you drink coffee or caffeinated sodas, take chocolate or tea to a lesser extent, eat sugar or other refined carbohydrates, eat sweet fruits or fruit without

If your liver is overworked, you will have anger, and if you have anger, you will trigger liver imbalances.

protein, or go without eating, you are asking your liver to work in a manner that is meant for emergencies only. The more you exhaust your liver, the more anger you will develop. This is true in Asian and Western medicine.

The Liver Has Three Basic Jobs

1. To remove toxins from your body

2. To aid in the digestion of fats and other food

3. To act as an emergency source of glycogen

This Shouldn't Be a Job for Your Liver

If your liver spends most of its time altering your blood sugar because you haven't eaten or you use caffeine or nicotine, it won't get the chance to do its other jobs. That can leave you filled with toxic material—the very thing that yeast loves to live on—and can interfere with your ability to break down fats, causing an overload in both your liver and gallbladder. Toxins in the body can cause you to become angry or nasty. Eventually your liver can become so overworked that it begins to be damaged as well.

"Oh, Kathleen, you won't believe what happened last weekend," Carol said to me. "My husband was having trouble with his stomach and his doctor thought it was an ulcer so she told him to drink cream and eat ice cream. Two days later he was in the bathtub trying to relax, and he called me to bring him something. I took one look at him and screamed. He was all yellow—his skin, the whites of his eyes, even his teeth looked yellow. I took him to the hospital, and he was diagnosed with a liver problem. He never had an ulcer at all. Later, he told me he had been jaundiced as a child. I was really scared."

The Alcohol Connection

Moderate alcohol use can damage your liver over a long period of time, whereas heavy drinking can damage your liver in a short period time. I have not discussed alcohol much in this book because it is in the same category as sugar and is treated the same way in your body. Most people are familiar with what alcohol abuse can do to a person's liver, and for that reason I decided not to dwell on alcohol abuse. But I want to point out that because alcohol use and abuse can affect your liver, and the liver is the seat of anger, it is highly suspect in any anger problem. In a study of alcohol abuse done in Germany at the Department of Medicine at the University of Heidleberg, alcohol use was found to be responsible for deaths from traffic accidents, violence, suicide, liver cirrhosis, cancer of the liver, stroke, alcoholic psychosis, and chronic pancreatitis.[5]

Toxic Waste

One day I saw Ben coming home from his university teaching position. He was holding a really mangled umbrella and muttering to himself. Every few steps he bashed the umbrella into a post or fence. He was angry! He was toxic! And he was muttering that he hadn't had a bowel movement yet. I knew what was causing his problem.

When your liver isn't working properly and you become toxic, a lot of things slow down in your system, especially your digestion and bowel movements. You also might get halitosis or bad breath because food is putrefying in your body due to poor digestion. Once your liver and gall-bladder start to underfunction, you can expect that your bowels will also slow down, causing constipation often alternating with diarrhea. You might have a metallic taste in your mouth when you wake up.

FEAR AND ANGER

Fear is often called "the great motivator," but it can also be the great killer as well. You've read earlier in this chapter that fear can and often does trigger the fight-or-flight syndrome or response. Fear has also been shown in recent research to cause death. Researchers at the University of San Diego even called their study "The Hound of the Baskervilles Effect."[6] (In the Sherlock Holmes novel *The Hound of the Baskervilles* people died from fear.) The results of this research showed that cardiac mortality increased in psychologically stressful occasions. In this particular case

Asian subjects reacted to fear of the number four as being unlucky. Since fear is known to trigger the fight-or-flight response, we can interpret this data to mean that fear contributed to these deaths by triggering the fight-or-flight response. Researchers took into account all the other factors such as changes in diet, alcohol intake, exercise, and drug regimens. What can we conclude from this study? It's so important to reduce fear, stress, and the fight-or-flight response if you want to remain not only healthy but also alive!

Karen lived in fear that Ann would beat her up on the way home from school all through grade school. Some days it actually happened; some days it didn't. After graduation from high school Karen worked in a nursing home. She was susceptible to all kinds of illnesses, including one that affected her immune system so much that she was hospitalized for months in isolation, lost her hair, and could barely function for several years. It took years of counseling and treatments to get Karen healthy

Workplace Stress and Violence

Workplace stress and cardiovascular deaths from workplace stress are increasing, yet even the Occupational Safety and Health Administration of the U.S. Department of Labor doesn't recognize poor nutrition or faulty lifestyle habits like skipping breakfast, caffeine and/or nicotine use, or sugar consumption as contributing to stress and violence in the workplace. Since 1981 I have been lecturing employees in corporations on the topic of "Food and Mood at Work" with great success. Many corporations now encourage their workers to follow the Anger Cure program. Workplace violence, anger, and personal downtime due to these factors are something I have been studying firsthand since 1989 when I ran a large insurance agency.

The main workplace stress that is recognized is either job strain (defined as high demands and low job control) and/or effort-reward imbalance (defined as high demands, low security, and few career opportunities). A study published in the October 2002 issue of *The British Medical Journal* concluded that workplace stress doubles the risk of death from heart disease.[7]

Cortisol/DHEA Ratio, Anger, and Stress

During stress, cortisol is secreted by the adrenal glands. Cortisol can be responsible for many different kinds of damage in the body when it is not in balance with dehydroepiandrosterone (DHEA). Research has shown that elevated cortisol/DHEA ratios in schizophrenic patients are positively associated with higher scores for anxiety and anger, depression and hostility unrelated to their psychopathology, or any antipsychotic treatment.[8]

Cortisol can be controlled by eating large amounts of sprouts from buckwheat, barley, fenugreek, and sunflower seeds, all of which contribute beta-sitosterols and beta-sitosterolins. Many supplements are also available that contain high amounts of this natural ingredient. In capsules or powder it is considered a whole food if it is from the sprout source. For more information on beta-sitosterols and beta-sitosterolins, see my website www.healthaliveproducts.com.

The Low Blood Sugar Test, the Syndrome X Test, and the Yeast Test all clearly show that anger is partly a nutritional problem that can be remedied. The Adrenal Function and Liver Function tests list symptoms of exhausted adrenals and liver and give you insight into why a faulty lifestyle can make you have angry reactions. Substances like caffeine, nicotine, alcohol, sugar, and refined carbohydrates are partly responsible for triggering anger attacks and the fight-or-flight response. Low amounts of B vitamins can contribute, as can low calcium and magnesium in your diet. Going without eating can also trigger the fight-or-flight syndrome, and this, in turn, can lead to anger, rage, violence, and depression.

Relaxation, exercise, and deep breathing are helpful in reversing the fight-or-flight reaction. It is also important to eat regular meals and avoid caffeine, nicotine, alcohol, sugar, and refined foods.

IS THERE A PILL?

There are many known nutrients from Western medicine and traditional Chinese medicine that function as adaptogens and help the body cope with stresses of all kinds. The adrenal glands are helped by vitamin B_5, licorice or its purified form glycyrrhizic acid, ginseng, adrenal extracts and, of course, small, frequent meals of lots of vegetables and small amounts of protein.

Liver problems are helped by artichoke, dandelion, milk thistle, N-acetyl cysteine, liver extracts, alpha-lipoic acid, bupleurum, and various digestive aids like betaine, hydrochloric acid, and enzymes. Generally, useful supplements have obvious names like liver support or hepato support (adrenal support, adreno, or adaptogen for supplements useful to the adrenals). A combination of Chinese herbs known as Sho-Saiko-To is reputed to dissolve liver tumors, inactivate viruses including hepatitis C, and restore liver function. Olive oil and olive leaf extract are helpful for good liver function. Olive leaf extract is known to be antiviral, antibacterial, and antiprotozoan, so it is useful if you have yeast problems, liver issues, or parasites.

CHAPTER SUMMARY

1. The fight-or-flight response is a reaction to assumed or real stress. In ancient times it was a survival mechanism; now it just weakens your body and creates more stress.

2. Your adrenal glands need to be healthy to withstand any stress. If not, you could experience rage, anger, violence, depression, low self-esteem, and illness.

3. Watching violence on TV, in the movies, at sports events, or in person in the street can increase your levels of anger, violence, rage, and hostility.

4. Your liver can be overworked by stress or fight-or-flight reactions, and this can lead to illness and anger.

5. Nutrition and specific supplements can help restore your adrenals and liver as well as help reverse anger reactions.

CHAPTER 9

What Throws You Off

*Bethany was a young college student when her boyfriend brought her to the
clinic where I worked. He was desperate because she was having mood swings,
angry episodes, and fatigue. His worst fear was that the phenobarbital she was
on because of her epilepsy was throwing her off and causing these problems.
But every time she tried to go off the medication she would get strange
symptoms so she went back on it. He was correct. She didn't have epilepsy;
she had a blood sugar imbalance brought on by an allergy to oranges.*

A lot of chemicals interact in your system, which sometimes creates
health problems. When this happens, drugs aren't the solution; you
have to get at the source of the problems. We discussed allergies in Chapter 2 along with using a rotation diet. Many more things can affect you that
may not be as obvious. I'm not going to discuss caffeine, nicotine, yeast, or
sugar here if I can help it because we've really covered them. If you feel
100 percent healthy, then you won't need to read this chapter. However, if
you have anger problems, fly off the handle, yell, lose your temper, or
have road rage, you need to read this chapter.

TIME TO DO SOME HOMEWORK

I have used the following system in personal counseling since 1983,
and it works. Keep a log of everything you put in your mouth and the time
you ate it, and a log of everything you feel and the time you felt it. Keep

two separate logs on one sheet of paper. If you eat one nut or jellybean, it goes down with the time. If you sneeze, itch, get angry, lose concentration—anything physical, mental, or emotional—it goes on the sheet. Do this for five days in a row. Pick days during the week and continue into the weekend if your routine is different, so you can compare your responses to different schedules. Make a separate chart for each day (see instructions below). The more details you are aware of and write down, the more likely it is you'll be able to get to the bottom of a problem. *Do not change or edit what you normally eat or do.* That would be akin to cheating on yourself. If you're interested in being totally healthy, that means no angry responses, no fatigue, no insomnia, no colds, no high or low blood pressure, no irregular heart beat, no violence, no runny nose, no hearing loss, no memory loss, no flying off the handle, no shaking of your knees, hands, or arms. Totally healthy.

Diet and Lifestyle Log

At the top left of the log put the date and day and then the time you got up and the time you went to sleep (see "Diet and Lifestyle Log—Example 1"). To clarify, this is not a log of eating something and seeing how you feel. It is two separate logs on the same page. Try to keep the times in order as if it were a date book or calendar. That way when you look for relationships you'll be able to find them easily. This record is just for you, so as long as you can read your own writing, you don't have to worry about typing it or rewriting it. You don't have to show it to anybody if you don't want to.

Every Detail

Watch yourself very closely and carefully. Note everything that happens and write it down next to the time it happens. Don't absently scratch your head and not write it down. Write down everything you do, say, or think that is not totally healthy. Itching, scratching, energy drops, anger— everything. If you notice a button has fallen off your coat and all you do is notice it, don't bother writing it down. If you notice it and you get upset about it, write it down. Note every twitch, twinge, and fear.

DIET AND LIFESTYLE LOG—EXAMPLE 1

Name _____   Date _____

Time Up: 7:00 A.M.   Time in Bed: 10:00 P.M.

TIME	ALL FOODS EATEN	TIME	ALL FEELINGS—PHYSICAL AND EMOTIONAL
7:00	Got up		
7:15	Coffee + double cream		
9:00	2 eggs (fried), white toast and butter		
		10:00	Yawning, sleepy
		10:45	Yelled at coworker for no reason
11:00	1 small apple		
		11:15	Headache better, legs itch
		12:30	Feeling touchy, felt like crying after call from tax dept. with bad news
		12:45	Feeling rushed, trouble concentrating
12:50	Cigarette		
1:00	Coffee + double cream		
		1:15	Nose running and itching, headache returning
1:20	2 aspirin		
1:45	2 muffins, wheat flour, sugar, and butter		
		2:00	Sleepy, need some fresh air, slight headache
		7:00	Feel groggy, slight headache

MY HIDDEN ALLERGY STORY

I had a problem all my life with my lungs. Most of the time I didn't know it was a problem. I couldn't run the bases when we played baseball in the empty lot across the street, but I thought that was because I was a girl. It was pretty flat in Michigan where I grew up, so riding my bike was no problem. It was actually easier than walking some of the time. We had a coal furnace, as did everybody in the neighborhood, as did my grade school. The only difference was that our home had forced air and the school had radiators. I used to come home from school feeling just fine and then suddenly have a runny nose, cough, earache, or shortness of breath. My mother, bless her heart, would always proclaim that I had a cold and couldn't go outside. I always responded by saying, "But I didn't have it at school. It must be something here." She would get all upset and say something like, "Are you trying to say my house isn't clean?" Well, it was the 1950s and women judged their success by a clean house. I was at a loss because I had no idea what to reply.

Can't Get the Breathing Correct

My main dream was to be a singer. I begged for lessons and finally got them when the voice teacher deemed my voice mature enough. I loved it, but there was something wrong. I couldn't get the breathing right. No matter what I did. I sang solos at school, did church solo work, and sang with a Tuesday Musicale group on Sundays. I was planning on being a classical singer. All this time my teacher kept insisting that I wasn't breathing correctly on purpose. I went to university and started as a music major, but I still couldn't get the breathing right. I was in folk opera and Italian and French operas, sang in various choirs, did solo work, earned my living singing at weddings, churches, and ladies' club meetings. So thinking I was stupid or incompetent, I gradually moved away from singing and got a degree in radio, TV, and journalism. I didn't have to worry about my breathing to write books. I loved it, too, but not like I loved singing.

Even Yoga Didn't Help the Breathing

I worked as a TV producer and did singing on the side in churches and choirs. Then I discovered health food. I felt a lot better eating nutritious food. I didn't wake up with a runny nose or cough every morning as I had done since I was a child. My voice was better than ever. I didn't have the sinus and/or mucus problems I'd been plagued with all my life. But I still couldn't get the breathing right, so I took yoga. I even became a yoga teacher, and I still couldn't get the breathing right. By now you must think something is missing in my brain. Finally, I moved to Santa Fe, New Mexico. The altitude is over 7,000 feet there, and the oxygen is sparse. Now I really couldn't get the breathing right, and a doctor declared that I might have asthma. Great, now I'll get the breathing right. But, nope, asthma medicine didn't help. I had to quit singing with the symphony because I couldn't hold a note. The conductor implied that I was untrained and that I could do better.

NAET/BioSet to the Rescue

Several years ago I decided to take a series of allergy tests and treatments called NAET/BioSet. After going once or twice a week for months, I finally discovered what caused my breathing problem. I was allergic to coal dust, and not only that, it was still lodged in my lungs from childhood. The young woman doing the test said, "It's so weird that you have this. Generally, people my mother's age have it." Then she looked at my chart and saw that I was her mother's age. Wow, what a compliment! She thought I was a lot younger than I really was. So she did the treatment, and lo and behold, I could sing. I finally got the breathing right. I'm happy I've found out what was wrong, but sorry that it took so many years of suffering from all kinds of weird diseases, not to mention about thirty collapsed lungs. It's too late for me to be a professional singer, but if it weren't for my breathing problem, I might never have become a nutritionist and helped thousands of people feel better and live happier lives.

> My Aunt May was over seventy years old when she turned to me one day and said, "I know why I've outlived all my brothers and sisters, even the younger ones."
>
> " Why is that?" I asked.
>
> "Because," she said with a twinkle in her eye, "I was really sick as a child, and I had to fight to stay alive, and now that is keeping me alive. They never had to fight, and they are all dead."

STOP RIGHT HERE AND DO YOUR DIET AND LIFESTYLE LOG

Do not read any further in this chapter until you have filled in five days (or more if you wish) of the Diet and Lifestyle Log, and have the finished sheets in front to you. Please do not read ahead. It might taint how you keep your log if you know what to look for while you're doing it.

DIETARY ERRORS

Start by lining up the pages of your Diet and Lifestyle Log in the order of the days. Have at least twenty different colors of pencils, pens, highlighters, or crayons available. There are twenty-two errors that you will be looking for, so noting each one with a different color will make it really easy to see. You may want to make a chart showing which color you used for which error so you'll know what you're doing later.

Now read the first error and circle every time you did it on your sheets. Do the same for all the errors. Note that I listed the easiest error first and then progressed to the more complicated ones. Don't be surprised if some of your meals have several different-colored circles on them.

ERROR 1: **Not eating within a half hour of getting up in the morning.** Look at each day and see what time you got up and what time you ate breakfast. If it is within a half hour, don't do anything. If it is not, circle it. If you had no breakfast at all, circle it. Do this for each day.

ERROR 2: **Taking stimulants.** This includes coffee, tea, chocolate, cigarettes, ephedra or guarana products, or anything with caffeine in it like colas. Circle every time you do this. Do this for each day.

ERROR 3: **Eating sweet foods.** This includes bananas, dried fruits, fruit juices, anything with sugar or honey in it, alcohol, or pastries or doughnuts. Caffeine-containing colas and other soft drinks go here, too. Circle every time you do this. Do this for each day.

ERROR 4: **Mixing fruits and grains at the same meal.** All breakfast cereals are grains; so is anything made of flour. So eating a bagel with strawberry jam qualifies as errors 3 and 4. Cereals with fruits in the box or added at the table qualify. Circle every time you do this. Do this for each day.

ERROR 5: **Mixing protein and grains at the same meal.** An egg and toast is mixing protein and grains. Chicken noodle soup is mixing protein and grains. Turkey with stuffing is mixing protein and grains. Sausage gravy and corn bread or biscuits is mixing protein and grains. Circle every time you do this. Do this for each day.

ERROR 6: **Going more than three to four hours without eating.** Just circle the hole and mark the time between eating. For example, put $4\frac{1}{2}$ in the circle if you go that long without eating. Circle every time you do this. Do this for each day.

ERROR 7: **Eating a big meal that you know is too much food.** I personally think that eating eggs, toast, and pancakes is too big a meal. Use that to judge how big is too big. If you feel stuffed, it is too big for sure. Circle every time you do this. Do this for each day.

ERROR 8: **Eating a big meal after not having eaten for six or more hours.** If you haven't eaten lunch and you eat a big dinner, that should be circled. If you haven't eaten all day and then you stuff yourself, that should be circled. Circle every time you do this. Do this for each day.

ERROR 9: **Eating too late at night–after 10 P.M.** This assumes you work from 8 to 6 or somewhere between those hours. Food eaten too late includes snacks and meals. If you're eating popcorn and pizza at midnight, that qualifies. Circle every time you do this. Do this for each day.

ERROR 10: **Eating your big meal after 7 P.M.** Circle every time you do this. Do this for each day.

ERROR 11: **Eating salty foods.** This includes the salt that you add to food as well as what's in foods like chips, canned soups, bacon, smoked meats, luncheon meats, or cheese. Circle every time you do this. Do this for each day.

ERROR 12: **Eating the same foods or drinks every day.** This can lead to a food sensitivity that can cause all kinds of health problems. Circle every time you do this. Do this for each day.

ERROR 13: **Eating fatty foods.** This includes butter, meats, cheese, cream, ice cream, whipped cream, cream sauces, bacon fat, and fatback. Circle every time you do this. Do this for each day.

ERROR 14: **Eating refined grains.** White bread, white rice, white flour pastas, pearl barley. Circle every time you do this. Do this for each day.

ERROR 15: No fresh fruit in any given day. This goes at the end of each day. If you haven't eaten any fresh fruit, write that in a circle. Circle every time you do this. Do this for each day.

ERROR 16: Eating too fast or not chewing each mouthful until it's liquid. Make a note in the circle when you notice yourself doing this. It might be hard to remember so late after making the log, but do the best you can. You may have written that you burped or had indigestion after a meal; that's from eating too fast or not chewing, and that should be in the log. Circle every time you do this. Do this for each day.

ERROR 17: Not eating whole grains. This means not eating 100 percent whole wheat, brown rice, millet, oats, barley, buckwheat, quinoa, rye, spelt, or Kamut. Circle every time you do this. Do this for each day.

ERROR 18: Eating allergy-causing foods. This includes oranges, dairy products, wheat, chicken or eggs, potatoes, or anything you already know you are either allergic or sensitive to, especially MSG, preservatives, additives, or chemicals like nitrates or sulfites. Circle every time you do this. Do this for each day.

ERROR 19: Eating yeast products or fermented foods. This includes bread with yeast, aged cheese, beer, wine, soy sauce, tempeh, Limburger cheese, blue cheese, pickles, vinegar and foods containing it like salad dressings, and perhaps sauerkraut. This also includes leftovers and foods that have been unrefrigerated for more than a half hour. Circle every time you do this. Do this for each day.

ERROR 20: Not eating enough vegetables. Six to ten servings a day is the best amount of vegetables to eat. One glass of veggie juice counts as one serving. Generally a serving is considered to be a half cup. At least one serving *must* be raw. So you have two things to mark here: not enough veggies and no raw veggies. Make a circle at the end of the day and write no veggies, not enough veggies, or no raw veggies in it. I'm always surprised to see that people often go days without eating any veggies at all. Circle every time you do this. Do this for each day.

ERRORS 21 & 22: **Not deep breathing while eating and not loving yourself while eating.** This is not a joke, though it's not something you may be able to look back on when you're analyzing your Diet and Lifestyle Log.

EMOTIONAL AND PHYSICAL SYMPTOMS

Now read through the emotional and physical symptoms listed below, and if any appear on your pages circle them there. You can use a different color for each one or highlight it. Since these are the symptoms and not the errors you just might want to circle them in all the same color. Here's what to look for:

Fatigue

Sleepiness

Anger or flying off the handle

Yelling at others

Depression or low self-esteem

Lack of concentration

Yawning

Confusion

Itching

Hair pulling

Mucus problems

Coughing

Nervous twitching

Any kind of twitching

Tapping your fingers or swinging your legs

Hair twiddling

Gum chewing

Staring off into space

Dropping things

Swelling

Highs and lows

Heart pounding or racing

Hands shaking

Stomach twinges or pain

Eye strain

Diarrhea or constipation

Bumping into things

Loss of balance or tripping

Unable to make a decision

Feeling of the bottom dropping out of your stomach

Rashes

Blurry vision

Feeling of being paralyzed

Memory loss

Inappropriate laughing

Anger or rage

Hitting someone or wanting to

Slamming things down

Slamming doors

Gunning the car engine needlessly

Drowsiness

Tingling in the extremities

Burping, belching, gas

Headaches

Backaches

Upset about your hair, nails, or other beauty problems

Now that you have circled all the dietary errors and the physical and emotional symptoms, we can start to get to the bottom of what aspects of your lifestyle aren't working for you and may be causing your anger, depression, fatigue, and lots of other health problems.

IS IT THE CHICKEN?

Connie was sent to me by a chiropractor who couldn't figure out what was wrong with her. After she filled in the Diet and Lifestyle Log, it was obvious that her main problem was that she kept dropping things, bumping into things, having dizzy spells, and had a lot of trouble with concentration and focus. When I first looked at her log, I could see that it only happened on Monday, Tuesday, and part of Wednesday, and always after eating Sunday dinner at her mother's. I started to think that I might have to refer her to a psychiatrist. When I looked at her log a little closer, I saw that every time she ate at her mother's she had a chicken dinner with mashed potatoes, gravy, peas, other veggies, salad, and fruit. I began to suspect the chicken until I noticed that on another day she had eaten a chicken salad sandwich and had none of the symptoms. Her log showed us that her problem was eating chicken and potatoes together. So, after making the discovery, she avoided the potatoes in the big Sunday chicken dinner and all her symptoms were gone.

SHE ONLY ATE PIE

A friend told me once that she only ate pie for Sunday night dinner. It sounded wonderful: whole-wheat crust with fresh apples, sunflower and pumpkin seeds, a drizzle of honey with an oatmeal-and-nut crumb topping that she piled high with natural yogurt. Everything was organic and natural. She started eating an entire 9-inch pie but developed trouble with digestion. She had burping, bloating, and sometimes even drowsiness afterward. Well, she loved it so much she kept eating it and thought she was just eating too much at once. After she'd cut back the amount week after week until she was only eating a small slice but still having problems, she asked me to figure out what was happening. She couldn't imagine what she was doing wrong since these were all considered healthy foods.

She didn't need to do the log; I knew right away what her problem was. She was mixing fruit, grains, and protein all in the same meal, and her body couldn't handle it. She could have stopped the yogurt or the pie altogether. But she chose the other option: She decided to take digestive enzymes and make sure she didn't go more than four or five hours without eating before she ate the pie. This woman had a lot of stress in her life, and her digestion was poor because of it, so she just couldn't handle the combination of these foods without digestive aids. I also suspected that she was sensitive to the lactose in dairy products, since she made the crust with butter and had yogurt with the pie. The digestive enzyme she took had lactase in it, and that solved all her digestion problems, including her problem with dairy.

Lactose is the sugar in dairy products. It is estimated that about 60 percent of all Caucasians and 80 to 90 percent of all Asians, Sephardic Jews, Africans, and people with these ethnic backgrounds cannot digest lactose or are intolerant to it.

HOW TO USE THE DIET AND LIFESTYLE LOG

Now that you've marked off all the dietary errors and all the physical and emotional things you experienced, you are ready to look at your charts to see what throws you off. Look at error 1 on your charts. Is there a similar reaction every time you make this error? Do you have allergies, scratch, itch, blow your nose, feel lethargic, have a headache, or get depressed? If so, you've found what throws you off. But don't stop here. Keep going through all the dietary errors. When you finish you will see exactly what throws you off and you will know exactly what to do to avoid the problem. If every time you go without eating and your blood sugar drops you are angry, you now know that this is what is throwing you off. If every time you eat oranges you get a headache, you now know what is throwing you off.

Look at "Diet and Lifestyle Log—Example 2" appearing on the next four pages to see how a log might look when it is marked up. (LBS is my abbreviation for low blood sugar and CHO is the general abbreviation for carbohydrates.)

DIET AND LIFESTYLE LOG—EXAMPLE 2

April 20th   Wake-up   4:40 am (return to bed)
                                   Get-up   9:50 am
                                   Go to bed 11:30 pm   *YEAST*

All day, acrid smell from my vagina. This has happened on-and-off all my life.

4:40	Small glass of orange juice cigarette *LBS*	Wake up: pain in calves, upper and lower back Sad about my failed romances
5:10		Gas Returned to bed
9:05	Wake up	Remember dreams of lost opportunities
9:20	Large apple	General stiffness
9:30	*LBS*	Scattered—race right by the door of chiropractor although I've been going there for months, I just don't know where the door is.
9:35	2 mouths of water	
10:30	Coffee/cream/sweetener cigarette	Sad, oppressed
10:45	Cigarette (still drinking the above coffee)	
11:00	Cigarette (same cup of coffee)	
11:30	Glass of water cigarette	
12:30	13 mini baby carrots 1/4 fennel bulb 1/2 chicken breast glass of water *too long to go*	Tightness in thighs, upper and lower back
12:55	Orange pekoe tea/sweetener/Lactaid cigarette	
1:00	Super ortivite 2 flaxseed oil caps taken with a mouthful of water *LBS*	Exhausted
1:30 2:15	1/2 glass of water *needs food* 1/2 glass of water	
3:00	1/2 glass of water	Following session with energy therapist, feeling less blocked

Marie's husband carried her into the clinic and put her in a chair one Friday afternoon. He said she was getting weaker and weaker all the time. He thought it was her diet.

"What are you eating?" I asked her.

"Peanut butter—that's all I can eat. I haven't eaten anything else for a few weeks."

"Are you getting weaker?"

"Yes, I can barely function and I'm a teacher."

"OK," I said, "don't eat peanut butter or peanuts at all; don't even touch them. I think you're allergic to them. Then come to my cooking class on Tuesday and I'll show you some new recipes that you'll be able to eat."

is she blood type A

3:20	Banana		Gas
3:40			Fearful about what I will do for dinner
4:05	Cigarette	*LBS*	Sore throat
4:10	Mouthful of water		
4:30	Multi-grain bagel		
5:30	Cranberry tea		
6:30	3 small slices of pizza topped with grilled chicken, tomato slices, black olives, garlic Small glass red wine	*digestion from LBS*	
7:30	Glass of water		
8:30			Bloated, tired
8:45	Glass of water Cigarette		Pain back, top of ribs—both sides, also neck stiffness
9:25	Imovane 7.5 mg Neurontin 400 mg Doxepin 50 mg ½ glass of water	*?*	Ache in both baby fingers
10:00			Heartburn
10:05	½ glass of ginger ale		
11:00	1 slice seed bread with almond butter 2 slices of seed bread with butter Glass of ginger ale	*starch & sugar*	

April 21st   Get-up   10:00 am
                 Go to bed   1:30 pm   *bed 11:30*

10:20	Glass of water		Sad
11:00	Coffee/cream/sweetener Cigarette		
11:15	Water		
	Cigarette		
11:30	Water		
	Cigarette	*too long to go*	Angry with Duncan.
1:00			Our relationship is obviously over (again). Angry that he won't confront what's going on —that he has let it slide through his fingers, that he used my energy to infuse his life.
1:30	Red river cereal with banana and 1½ tsp maple syrup		
1:40			Call Duncan to lash out but left frustrated and still angry. Although I tell him I'm not available to support him, I know it's not true.

"Fine," Marie's husband replied, "I'll see that she does it." And he carried her out of the office.

Tuesday a stranger came to my cooking class late. "Hi, may I help you?" I asked.

"Yes," was her reply, "I'm here for the class. I registered."

"You registered on the telephone? You don't look familiar."

"No, I registered in person last week. I'm the one who used to only eat peanut butter. I started to eat real food and gave up the peanut butter, and I'm feeling great now. You saved my life."

Time	Food/Drink	Symptom/Note
1:55	Orange pekoe tea/sweetener/2% Lactaid Cigarette	Feeling powerless in face of Duncan's intransigence
3:00	*LBS*	Sexually aroused
3:10	1/2 cup of coffee/sweetener/cream Cigarette	
4:00		Emotionally dead
4:20	Glass of water Cigarette	
5:00	Glass of water Cigarette	
6:00	*too long to go*	Sharp lower back pain and buttock pain (right side)
6:25	Glass of water	
6:50	Yam with Tbsp tahini and Tbsp yogurt (1%)	
7:30	Cigarette	
7:45	Ginger ale Cigarette	
9:00		Neck very tight *LBS*
9:05	5 mini baby carrots 1 cup chicken broth 9 angelotti stuffed with ricotta and sun-dried tomatoes 1 1/2 cup salad (spinach and bean sprouts) 1 Tbsp dressing (olive oil and raspberry vinegar with mustard)	
10:30	Cigarette	Gas
10:40		Sneeze
10:45		Conversation with Janice who tells me I've done harder things than taking care of myself/ getting my food under control. I don't agree.
11:35	Imovane 7.5 mg Neurontin 400 mg Doxepin 50 mg 1/2 glass of water Mouthful of ginger ale	*groggy from*
Midnight	4 mini baby carrots (organic) 2 slices rye sunflower toast with almond butter (organic)	*Cho & yeast*
1:30	Ginger ale	Fell asleep watching television

LBS   *too sweet*

THROW OUT WHAT'S THROWING YOU OFF

The Diet and Lifestyle Log will help you pinpoint exactly what is throwing you off. You might be triggered into angry responses by low blood sugar, a yeast overgrowth, Syndrome X, going too long without eating, or food allergies. Once you see the similarities between what you eat or don't eat and the times you eat or don't eat and all the different symptoms that you experience, you can begin to eliminate those offending foods, drinks, or habits.

April 22nd   Get-up   11:05 am   (Sharp pain in lower back) *LBS*
                                              Sneeze
                                              Pain inner arch of left foot
                                              Both feet—dull ache

                        Go to bed 12:15 am

11:30	Small glass guava/strawberry/apple juice Medium Lactaid Cappuccino/sweetener/cinnamon (sipped over two hours) Cigarette	*No real food!*
11:45	Cigarette	
1:30	1/2 glass water	Pain in lower back continues Don't know what to do next
1:35	Cigarette	*LBS*
1:45	Glass of water Cigarette	
3:00	1 1/2 cup Salad (spinach/fennel/bean sprouts) with can or water packed tuna 1 Tbls dressing (olive oil, raspberry vinegar)	*finally food at 3:00*
3:20	Orange pekoe tea (sweetener) Lactaid Cigarette	*got up at 11:00* *4 hours*
3:45	Cigarette	
4:30	1 piece Arm & Hammer dental care gum	Obsessed with Duncan, can't keep from thinking about him
5:15	Cigarette	
6:00	Glass of water	
7:00	Ginger ale	After a walk of 1 hour, balls of feet burning, all over body pain particularly calves and hip flexors
7:30	Smoke small joint	
8:00	3 small lamb chops 6 asparagus tips baked in (balsamic vinegar) 3/4 cup yams baked with butter and (brown sugar) 3/4 cup salad (mixed greens and toasted sunflower seeds) with vinaigrette dressing	*Yeast*

Monosodium Glutamate

Monosodium glutamate (MSG) presents a really tricky problem. Since MSG is an excitotoxin, it may react in such a way in your brain to cause mood swings, violent acts, depression, and anger. And it may be in a lot of food you don't suspect. We think of it mostly in Chinese food, but it's in a lot more than that. In the 1950s and 1960s many people used a food flavor enhancer called Accent, which was mostly MSG. In a Seventh Day Adventist cookbook from the 1970s MSG was used extensively; it was declared to be safe by the National Academy of Sciences/National Research Council. The MSG they were using was said to be similar to the amino acid compounds found in wheat, soybeans, and meat.[1]

Other flavor enhancers used in foods and listed on labels may also
signify that MSG is in the food. According to Dr. George Schwartz in his
book *In Bad Taste: The MSG Syndrome* (1988) or the revised edition *In Bad
Taste: The MSG Symptom Complex* (1999), MSG is often called hydrolyzed
vegetable protein (HVP) or it is listed as "seaweed extract" on food labels.
MSG might also be listed as hydrolyzed protein, hydrolyzed plant protein, plant protein extract, sodium caseinate, calcium caseinate, yeast
extract, texturized protein, or autolyzed yeast.

More and more people are becoming sensitive to MSG because it is in
so many foods. Read the labels on any packaged or canned soup you purchase in the grocery store. It is difficult to find any soup, canned or dry,
without it. Read the labels on any packaged, canned, frozen, or prepared
foods to see if they contain any of the ingredients known by the different
names used for MSG. If you want to be healthy and eliminate anger and
rage from your life, please don't ingest foods or drinks with any form of
MSG in them.

People Are Shocking

One Saturday I was doing a cooking demonstration of how to use tofu.
A woman approached me to do nutrition counseling for her university-
aged daughter. Her daughter was getting weaker and weaker and was
sleeping more and more, and the mother was afraid she might fail school.
I had the daughter fill in a Diet and Lifestyle Log, we
did a hair analysis, and she took the same
tests you've already taken in this book.
The daughter was very bright, and she
was also upset that her mother was
worrying about her so much. She just
figured that she had been studying too
hard and that when her classes were over

The more food she ate as the days went by, the more symptoms she exhibited. She was fatigued, vague, had confusion, exhaustion, and dizzy spells.

she could get some decent sleep and have her
energy back. I asked her when she first started to feel vague. "Right after
they took me to the hospital when I had the problem in the Chinese
restaurant. I've never been the same since." She began to get ill in a Chinese restaurant. Bingo! MSG problems.

I looked at her food and could see that her mother was making her eat frozen meals. The more food she ate as the days went by, the more symptoms she exhibited. She was fatigued, vague, had confusion, exhaustion, and dizzy spells. So I asked to see the frozen meals. They all had MSG in them. So I took the mother aside and said, "You have to stop giving her these frozen meals; they're what's making her ill."

I'm not kidding that the mother looked at me with a shocked look and said, "I can't do that. They cost me a lot of money. I can't just throw food out. Once she's eaten them all I'll stop buying them. She needs to eat something."

"Yes," I said, "but not these meals. They are making her ill. She is reacting to the MSG in them. That is all that's wrong with her. It could kill her if you keep it up."

"Well," she sighed, "once they're gone, I won't get any more."

I couldn't believe it! So I said to her, "Do you mean to tell me that you would risk your daughter's life by giving her these meals rather than throwing them out and saving her?"

"Well, my husband and I will eat them then."

I told the daughter to stop eating the frozen meals, and she recovered in a few days.

MSG and Anger

A study published in 2004 in the journal *Food Chemistry Toxicology* showed that rats fed a hypercaloric diet and MSG developed hyperinsulinemia and hyperglycemia and failed an oral glucose tolerance test. This means that giving them a high-calorie diet containing MSG–which is exactly what most people who lead a fast-food lifestyle eat–can cause two different kinds of blood sugar problems.[2] And blood sugar problems, we have already learned, will cause anger.

MSG and Obesity

According to an article posted on www.rense.com entitled "MSG–Slowly Poisoning America," MSG has been known to cause obesity since at least 1978 when research was published detailing how MSG was used to make rats obese for research. Studies backing this up are mentioned in *The*

Slow Poisoning of America by John Erb and T. Michelle Erb (Paladins Press, 2003; available at www.spofamerica.com). It's clear then that high-calorie, high-density, high-sodium fast foods and prepackaged and prepared foods that contain MSG will make people fat if they eat them on a regular basis.

MSG also has the tendency to make people overeat because it is addictive. The more you eat MSG, the more you want foods with MSG. The larger amount of food you consume, the more obese you become. The more obese you become, the more chances you have of throwing off your blood sugar and exhibiting type 2 diabetes symptoms.

SECRET INFORMATION

This chapter covers all my secret information. You now know how to determine what throws you off using the same system I've used for my clients for nearly thirty years. Please use this information to help heal your body and become totally healthy and anger-free. However, if after following the Anger Cure diet, adding supplements, and making lifestyle changes you're not completely free of anger, you may want to seek the help of a certified medical practitioner. I would suggest, among many, a homeopathic physician, a holistic allergist, an environmental medicine specialist, and of course a psychologist or psychiatrist. You may have any number of emotional situations that need to be resolved before you can be truly anger-free.

CHAPTER SUMMARY

1. Keeping a Diet and Lifestyle Log is a good way to determine what throws you off and contributes to health problems and anger.

2. Many physical and emotional problems can be overcome once you learn the diet or lifestyle errors that contribute to it.

3. It is up to you to take action and throw out the foods and habits that are throwing you off.

CHAPTER 10

The Anger Cure Program

Peter was on disability from his job because of panic attacks, anger, and rage. He was a skilled artist and used this time to get commissions from corporations for the large paintings he liked to do. He smoked several packs of cigarettes, drank about 5 quarts of coffee each day, and was almost impossible to talk to. You never knew when he might flare up and launch an angry attack. Once he flew into a rage and had to be held back by three men.

We were all praying for his healing, and one night even he prayed for healing from cigarettes. He woke up the next morning with no desire to smoke at all. Then he gave up coffee after much insisting and cajoling from me. A few weeks later he started to eat breakfast. He was a completely changed man. No more angry shouting. No more flying into a rage. We were no longer afraid of him and what he might do if he got upset. He couldn't get his doctors to believe that giving up coffee and cigarettes and eating breakfast had healed his anger, rage, and panic attacks, but we all knew it was the first step in his healing.

Twenty years have passed since I saw Peter become a totally stable person from some simple dietary changes. The Anger Cure worked for him. This chapter gives you all the information you will need to follow the Anger Cure program and liberate yourself from anger, rage, fatigue, depression, and a host of other health problems that you thought you would "just have to live with." The only "self-control" most people need is to eat frequently and follow the Anger Cure program.

YOU CAN FIND FREEDOM

Being healthy is freedom. Freedom from pain, fatigue, low self-esteem, rage, and anger. Freedom to do what you want and not be held back by poor health or fear. Try the program for a month and see how you feel. Once you take the supplements recommended in the earlier chapters and follow the diet recommendations here, you will find a big difference in *you*. It may take a few days to notice changes, or it may take six months, but you will notice changes. Get your friends and family to support you in making these changes and in assessing your progress.

Pain Is Easily Forgotten

You only remember pain when it's bugging you. Once it's no longer in your life, it will not seem as if you had any pain. (The pain I'm referring to can be physical or mental; most of the tests in this book cover both aspects of health.) Many people only remember the pain of today or yesterday, not three weeks ago. So I have people say to me, "This diet and/or supplements aren't working. I still have pain." When I quiz them further, it's obvious they started with a pain level of twenty and now have only a level of eight. They don't remember the twenty; they just want to get to zero, and the level of pain at eight seems like nothing has happened. I have met dozens of people who are content to walk around with pain at a level of twenty because they can't believe anything can be done. If only they tried the diet and supplements, they would be free of pain today. Look at all the tests you've taken to review your symptoms of pain and where they originate. You will also see how you acquired the anger syndrome.

Which One Will You Feed?

An old Cherokee is telling his grandson about the fight that is going on inside himself. The fight is between two wolves. One wolf is represented by anger, envy, sorrow, regret, greed, arrogance, self-pity, guilt, resentment, inferiority, lies, false pride, superiority, and ego. The other is filled with joy, peace, love, hope, generosity, humility, kindness, benevolence, empathy, truth, compassion, and faith in humankind.

The grandson asks, "Which wolf wins, grandfather?"

The simple reply was, "The one I feed."

Like the old Cherokee, you have a choice of which wolf you will feed. Will you continue with anger, envy, sorrow, regret, and all those other characteristics the old man named or will you feed joy, peace, love, hope, and positive characteristics? When you feed yourself the foods and supplements recommended, you will be feeding the positive side of yourself. You will be so strong the negative side will not have a chance of emerging.

ORANGES STOP THIEVERY was the headline on the little newspaper clipping from England my client brought me. The article reported that if people ate oranges before they went shopping, it would reduce stealing. When your blood sugar drops, you may have trouble telling right from wrong or you might be looking for a thrill and steal something. Eating oranges would bring up blood sugar for an hour or more so the person could shop and think morally.

STEP BY STEP

The Anger Cure can be followed all at once or step by step. It's up to you which one you choose. Everybody is different and has a different level of tolerance for change. If you can make a big change easily and do it all at once, that is best because you will see results sooner. If you want to make small changes over a longer period, that is fine, too. I'm going to outline the step-by-step plan first and then the complete plan. Choose whichever one suits you.

Start with the easiest step first. If you don't normally eat breakfast, start with that. After a few days of eating breakfast, add the next step and continue until you are following the total program. It may only take a few days to notice a change or it may take six months. Enlist the help of your friends and family to work with you. They may notice subtle changes in you long before you do.

Step 1

Eat breakfast. Start each day with breakfast. It's ideal to eat within the first half hour of getting up. At first, if you wish, just eat something for breakfast to get in the habit of doing it. Then eat a proper breakfast—one without sugar or refined carbohydrates, caffeine, or nicotine. Try to overcome the idea you learned as a child that breakfast had to be sweet to be good. When you feel great because you have eaten a good breakfast, you will let that idea go. Once you have mastered this step and are comfortable with it go on to the next step.

Step 2

Eat every three to four hours. The ideal to balance your body is to eat enough food at each meal to last for three to four hours. Then eat again. Doing this can go a long way toward preventing cravings for caffeine, nicotine, and sugar. When done regularly, this can also prevent triggering anger, rage, depression, and low self-esteem.

Carry food with you in little baggies to snack on. Good choices include nuts (you only need four or five almonds or walnuts for a snack), veggie sticks, non-aged cheese cubes, small cans of veggie juice, or sunflower and pumpkin seeds. Once you have mastered this step and are comfortable with it go on to the next step.

Step 3

Don't eat after 7:30 at night. Do not eat a big meal, sweet snacks, or fatty or rich foods after 7:30 P.M. If you must have a snack after 7:30 P.M., have a half of a piece of fresh fruit with some protein like a few nuts, peanut or almond butter, or a small amount of real cheese. Once you have mastered this step and are comfortable with it go on to the next step.

Step 4

Eat only whole grains. Replace all the white bread, pasta, cereal, rice, and flour products with whole-grain products. Eat only 100 percent whole-grain bread and use 100 percent whole-wheat flour for muffins, biscuits, and gravy. Eat only brown rice and be sure to ask for it when you're eating out; many Chinese and Japanese restaurants have it now. Eat whole oatmeal, not instant. Once you have mastered this step and are comfortable with it go on to the next step.

Step 5

Chew each mouthful until it is liquid in your mouth. Start by counting the number of times you chew a mouthful, and then make an effort to chew a mouthful at least twenty-five times. If that isn't enough to make it liquid, chew it until it is liquid. Take a digestive enzyme with each meal if you need it. Once you have mastered this step and are comfortable with it go on to the next step.

Step 6

Stop using caffeine. Switch to decaffeinated beverages if you can, or start by mixing half coffee, tea, or chocolate with half decaf. After a few days or a week switch to only decaf. Decaf is not 100 percent caffeine-free, so you will want to give up decaf eventually as well. Once you have mastered this step and are comfortable with it go on to the next step.

Step 7

Trade in your sweetened foods for nonsweetened foods. If you drink soft drinks or sugary drinks, switch to diluted fruit juice or veggie juice. Or you could try water or water with lemon. Remember no ice either. Instead of ice cream have unsweetened natural yogurt with berries. As a first step, use the kind of jam that has no sugar but is sweetened with fruit juice and then go off jam altogether. Have almond or peanut butter on toast or bagels instead of jelly or jam. Instead of a candy bar or muffins have some cheese and veggies or some nuts and a small amount of fresh fruit like a third of an apple or pear. Instead of pieces of candy have some sticks of carrots, celery, or red peppers.

Use a blood sugar supplement to help with the cravings. Try not to chew gum at all or switch to xylitol-sweetened gum and slowly stop using it. Once you have mastered this step and are comfortable with it go on to the next step.

Step 8

Exercise every day. Start with walking and deep breathing as outlined in Chapter 3. Add in more vigorous exercise like bicycling, swimming, dancing, or skating once you have gotten in shape. Once you have mastered this step and are comfortable with it go on to the next step.

Step 9

Stop using nicotine. By now your desire for nicotine should be about nil. However, if you are still smoking, begin to reduce the number of cigarettes and the frequency of your intake. Look at when you want cigarettes the most and determine why you are smoking. Research has shown that most people equate smoking with drinking alcohol or coffee, and since you have given those up, there must be some other reason for wanting cigarettes. Once you have mastered this step and are comfortable with it go on to the next step.

Step 10

Eat more vegetables, six to ten servings a day. When you have two snacks of vegetables and vegetables for lunch and dinner, you are most likely getting six servings. Make sure at least one serving is raw. Try having veggies for breakfast; leftover veggies are great in an omelet, with fried brown rice, or in a soup or stew. Veggie juice with unsweetened protein powder or tofu makes a great breakfast with veggies. Once you have mastered this step and are comfortable with it go on to the next step.

Step 11

Reduce or eliminate carbohydrates. Eating carbohydrates can often trigger blood sugar crashes and yeast growth—the two things that can easily lead to angry actions and reactions. This means no potatoes, grains of any kind, most fruits and fruit juices, no food with breading on it, nothing like beer or wine, no dried fruits, and nothing with sugar or flour. Don't forget that crackers, pretzels, chips, muffins, cookies, pancakes, and buns are all made from refined and processed wheat flour. If you really want to have pasta, have a high-protein pasta (as noted on the label), *saifun* (Oriental bean thread noodles), or baked or boiled spaghetti squash. Use a blood sugar supplement to help with the cravings.

Note: I put this step almost last because this is the very last step in keeping your energy levels constant: no highs and no lows. If you finished with the first ten steps and you feel really great and have no anger situations in your life anymore, you may not need to do this step.

Once you have mastered this step and are comfortable with it go on to the next step.

Step 12

Do not drink beverages with ice in them. Ice can shock your digestive system and start the fight-or-flight syndrome. The only acceptable time to have ice water is during the heat of summer, if you get too hot working out or riding your bike, or any time you are really heated up.

Step 13

Practice the anger management techniques outlined in Chapter 11.

MIX AND MATCH

You can mix and match the steps in any way you like. I arranged them to start with the easiest and progress to the most difficult. It's up to you. Do them in any order you want. You can do two at once, like eating breakfast and switching to whole grains. A nice breakfast of oatmeal with some steamed veggies and butter sounds really great to me; that would take care of steps 1 and 4. Add in chewing and you have three steps at once.

THREE DAYS TO FOURTEEN WEEKS

You might choose to progress through the steps at a pace that takes three days or three weeks. You might even take up to fourteen weeks. It's up to you. The one thing you don't want to do is cause yourself stress by forcing your body—or your mind for that matter—to do something it's not ready to do. It's more important to think of making these changes as a long-term commitment. So often when people jump into a program, they jump out just as fast. Gradually making changes suits most people and allows them to adjust so they can maintain a healthy program for a lifetime.

So often when people jump into a program, they jump out just as fast. Gradually making changes suits most people and allows them to adjust so they can maintain a healthy program for a lifetime.

NOW DO ANOTHER DIET AND LIFESTYLE LOG

Once you've been doing all the steps for a month or so and feel comfortable with how your program is going, do another Diet and Lifestyle Log. Fill it in for five days, mark it according to the instructions, and assess how you look and feel. Now you can see how the Anger Cure changes have helped your mood, anger response, depression, fatigue, or whatever your complaint was. Something you never knew you had may have cleared up, too.

KEEP A JOURNAL

The ideal way to keep track of what triggers your anger is to keep a journal. Whenever you have an angry outburst, flare-up, or even feel angry, write it down and look back over the day or the previous two days to see if you have committed any of the dietary errors that allowed your body to get out of balance and become angry. Now don't get me wrong: There is nothing wrong with becoming angry when something really merits it, as long as you don't either internalize it or strike out at someone verbally or physically. If an incident makes you angry one day and not another, you can be sure your lifestyle is involved. It often takes several days of following the Anger Cure program before your body is back to being balanced. So if you find that on Tuesday you yelled at someone and on the Saturday before that you drank a few beers or soft drinks, you'll be able to see a pattern of what throws you off. Don't get upset about it. Just make a note to not make that dietary error again, or realize that when you do something that triggers anger, you need to watch yourself very closely so that you don't act out and become angry.

> Billy came to me because he was having trouble staying awake in his training sessions. He had failed a test to become an insurance agent in a new state after being one for ten years. Now he was going to a self-directed school, sitting in a room with a textbook and tape player, and studying. But he kept falling asleep and was very upset about it. Billy had been eating carbohydrate snacks like pretzels and crackers because he'd discovered over the years that he felt better when he ate them. He hadn't noticed that they also made him sleepy. So he went on the Anger Cure program and was delighted to notice

that not only did he stay awake but also he was more alert and had fewer angry outbursts. This time when he took the test, he received 100 percent; in fact, Billy was the first person in the history of the state to get that honor. Billy's wife was also happy about his new attitude toward life. She called to tell me how much easier it was to live with him. Before she had to keep alert so she wouldn't say something that might trigger an angry outburst. Now she could just be herself.

MEALS ARE INTERCHANGEABLE

All the meals suggested in the Anger Cure program (see below) are

---

The Anger Cure Daily Plan

Eat breakfast within a half hour of getting up.

   OR

Drink vegetable juice or have a piece of low-glycemic index fruit.

Exercise.

(Do not take caffeine or nicotine.)

Breakfast should be protein and vegetables.

Drink water.

Two to three hours later have a non-carbohydrate snack.

Drink water.

Two to three hours later eat lunch.

Drink water.

Two to three hours later have another snack.

Drink water.

Two to three hours later eat dinner.

(If it is after 7 P.M. when you eat, eat a light meal.)

Drink water.

Exercise now if you didn't do it earlier, or do more.

Spend time with your family and friends.

Two to three hours after dinner have a light snack.

(Do not have a snack if you are going to bed within an hour of this time.)

Drink water.

Go to bed.

interchangeable. You can eat any meal at any time of the day. If you want to just have the snacks and no meals, that's fine, too. Just remember to eat every two to three hours as outlined in the Anger Cure daily plan. Many people need to eat a little something every two hours. Never go more than three or four hours without eating. That can put you into distress and cause anger, cravings, insomnia, and all kinds of problems. The days when you want the coffee, cigarette, or sugar items are often the days you didn't eat all the meals and snacks or didn't eat correctly the day before.

If you get home from work and all you have time for is a protein shake, go for it. That is better than not eating at all. If you have to grab something to eat in the car, get an apple and some nuts or cheese cubes and veggie sticks.

Following are the Anger Cure suggested meals. An asterisk (*) indicates that there is a recipe for that meal in Appendix B.

Suggested Meals

BREAKFAST
Choose from the following breakfast options.

- Two soft-boiled eggs with parsley, butter, and garlic
- Oatmeal with broccoli, ginger, garlic, and olive oil or butter*
- Scrambled eggs (2) with mushrooms, onions, garlic, red peppers, and parsley or other fresh herbs
- Stir-fried chicken livers with red and green peppers, onions, garlic, and ginger*
- One small lamb chop, broiled
- One small pork chop, broiled

- A 4-ounce piece of steak, liver, chicken, or thick-cut bacon and lettuce or other vegetable
- Chopped veggies and unsweetened yogurt
- Protein shake* with no sweetener, and a small amount of low-glycemic fruit if desired, using soy or dairy milk or tofu
- Salmon, tuna, or egg salad with onion, garlic, red peppers, parsley, and mayonnaise on a bed of lettuce
- Leftover meats and veggies

- Steamed veggies and a boiled egg with olive oil or butter and garlic* (one small potato can be used here along with broccoli, green beans, cabbage, kale, sweet potatoes, and so on)
- Cottage cheese and low-glycemic fruits
- Cottage cheese with chopped fresh herbs
- Meat and vegetable soup or stew*
- Fried brown rice with meat or eggs and veggies*
- High-protein pasta soup and veggies*
- Scrambled tofu with onions, red peppers, and broccoli*
- Egg Foo Yung*

SNACKS ANY TIME

Choose from the following snack options.

- Sunflower and pumpkin seeds with walnuts (not roasted or salted)
- Raw veggie sticks: cucumber, red or green peppers, zucchini, broccoli stems, kohlrabi, turnip, sweet potato, green onion, parsley
- Cheese sticks, unprocessed cheeses
- Hard-boiled egg and veggies
- Mixed veggie juice
- Unsweetened yogurt
- Unsweetened yogurt with chopped cucumber, cumin, and fresh mint
- Unsweetened protein shake*
- Lettuce roll-ups*
- Half an apple and cheese or nuts
- Stuffed celery*
- Brazil nuts and walnuts (especially if you have depression)
- Cream cheese and sprout balls*
- One rice cake with nut butter or cheese on it
- Six to ten fresh cherries with sunflower seeds
- Half a fresh pear with cheese, cream cheese, or nuts
- Half a fresh grapefruit
- Veggie sticks with guacamole dip*

LUNCH

Choose from the following lunch options.

- Green salad with chicken
- Unsweetened yogurt and veggies
- Jamaican black bean soup*
- Stuffed pepper* or cabbage
- Egg Foo Yung*
- Beef stew*
- Cottage cheese, cucumbers, cumin, and fresh mint salad
- Chopped egg salad with onion, garlic, green olives, and parsley on leaf lettuce
- Stuffed avocado*

- Two hard-boiled eggs and veggie sticks
- Salade Niçoise*
- Tuna salad* with one brown rice cracker
- Lettuce roll-ups* and veggie sticks
- Creamed chicken soup*
- Tempeh and green bean stew
- Tofu salad* with leaf or romaine lettuce
- Veggie sticks and black bean tofu dip*

DINNER

Choose from the following dinner options.

- Chef's salad with oat bran muffin*
- Four ounces of baked or broiled meat, and low-glycemic veggies
- Lentil and meat stew* with salad
- Cabbage salad meal*
- Stuffed pepper* or cabbage

- Waldorf salad meal* on leaf or romaine lettuce
- No-nitrate hot dog with spelt bun, sauerkraut, mustard, leaf lettuce
- Stuffed avocado* on leaf lettuce
- Baked sweet potato with butter and green salad with olive oil and lemon dressing

- Jamaican black bean soup* and green or cabbage salad

- High-protein macaroni and cheese with veggies*

- Stir-fried chicken livers with red and green peppers, and garlic and ginger* with saifun or spaghetti squash

- Egg Foo Yung* with saifun or spaghetti squash

- Cheese omelet and salad

- Asparagus omelet and Middle Eastern cucumber salad*

- Italian tomato and mozzarella salad,* steamed green beans and sweet potato

- Chicken Waldorf salad* on leaf lettuce

- Four ounces of broiled or baked meat, and oven-roasted veggies*

- Creamy chicken and tomato soup*

- Mushroom and barley soup* with cottage cheese salad

- Salade Niçoise*

- Slice of roast pork with baked apples* and steamed Brussels sprouts with lemon and butter

Plan Ahead

You must plan ahead to follow the Anger Cure eating plan. Always have hard-boiled eggs and veggie sticks on hand. Always have unroasted, unsalted mixed nuts and seeds around for snacking. (Keep them in little baggies in the freezer for emergency snacks.) Don't plan a large meal on a night you know you have to work late unless you can get the stove or a slow cooker to do the work while you're on the way home; that way you won't be eating too late at night. Always make sure you have breakfast foods that are fast if you need them, so you're not tempted to eat a doughnut or pick up a coffee out of convenience.

ADDING THE SUPPLEMENTS

If you're really out of balance and you know it, you may want to start with the supplements (mentioned throughout the book; see Chapters 2, 4, 5, 6, 9, and Appendix A) and the step-by-step plan. Or you may want to try the diet first and then add the supplements later. The supplements can help you avoid cravings and keep your energy levels stable. Almost every person who has consulted me about supplements and/or health needs digestive enzymes (see Chapter 4). I take them myself at every meal but not with snacks. I also take a blood sugar supplement if I'm under stress. At first I took these supplements faithfully for several months, and now I just take them when I feel I need them. As always, if you are currently under a doctor's care, please check with him or her before taking any supplement. Do not stop any medication without permission.

LET ME HEAR FROM YOU

Stories of how this information helped you are always welcome. You may share them on my website: www.angercure.com. Just click on the button "Testimonials" and leave your story.

CHAPTER SUMMARY

1. Follow the step-by-step plan and add in the supplements recommended throughout the book. It may take a few weeks before you're able to work it all into a natural flow in your life.

2. The thirteen steps can be followed in any order or combination.

3. Who said breakfast has to be sweet? It shouldn't be if you want to maintain your energy and be healthy all day.

4. Always carry approved snacks with you or know when and where to get some.

CHAPTER 11

The Body/Mind Connection

"But, Kathleen, it can't be all nutrition!" a new student exclaimed.

"You are so correct. There is more to it," I answered. "There is the body/mind connection that can help make your program easier to follow and train your mind to develop a new habit of transforming anger into peace and love."

Your body takes instructions from your mind. Unfortunately for most modern North Americans, their minds give the wrong information to their bodies because of nutritional and metabolic imbalances, as we've seen in the first ten chapters of this book. Recent work by Bruce Lipton, Ph.D., in his newest book, *The Biology of Belief* (Mountain of Love/Elite Books, 2005) has shown that we are complicated beings controlled even at the genetic/cellular level by our minds. So the old adage, "Change your mind, change your body," is actually true according to Lipton's new biological findings.

Yoga instructors have been teaching this for more than 3,000 years, and now science is showing that it's true. There truly is a body/mind connection. In the 1970s biofeedback was popular. This is a body/mind relaxation technique using a machine to detect stress in the body. The biofeedback machine, often called a galvanic skin-response machine because it measures the stress levels on the skin of the fingers, emits a high-pitched sound that gradually becomes softer and lower pitched as you train yourself to relax. When total relaxation is accomplished, no sound comes from the little machine.

Some of the biofeedback machines were very sophisticated and could actually detect various brain waves. Alpha is the brain wave of meditation, beta is the brain wave of daily life, and delta and gamma are the brain waves of inspiration and deeper spiritual states. With these machines it was possible to practice any brain wave so you could easily repeat it at will.

Some of the biofeedback machines trained the practitioner to heat up a hand or calm jerking muscles, even stop a muscle spasm that was the start of a heart attack. It was very effective for the people who actually practiced it. During the height of its popularity some people called biofeedback "yoga of the West" because it was the same kind of body/mind practice that Eastern yogis and yoginis practiced.

> A relative of mine, so the story goes, used the body/mind connection to save her son's life. She looked out the window and saw him working on his car. Suddenly the car started to slip and was about to crush him so she ran out, without thinking, and lifted the car off him. Her mind gave the instructions to her body to have that burst of energy—using the fight-or-flight syndrome we talked about in Chapter 8—and the confidence to actually do something that her regular waking mind would never have attempted.

Any habit can be changed by following a few easy steps, which we will outline in this chapter. Since your mind and body work together, you will want to make the nutritional changes and also do the mind exercises for the best results in overcoming anger and rage.

STEPS TO CHANGE A HABIT

It might take you a few days or weeks to master each of these steps, and that's OK. How long have you had this anger problem? You can't expect something that you've had for years to go away in a day or so. Be patient with yourself. As you change your diet, add in these steps and mind exercises. That way you will have a total body/mind change.

Step 1

Recognize the habit. First you have to recognize that you have the habit in order to change it. Since you are reading this book, you have already recognized that you have a habit of anger and/or rage.

Step 2

Recognize doing it. When you have anger, recognize that you are practicing this habit at the time you are actually in the midst of it. How does it feel? Observe how it looks to you and to others. Feel how you feel while being angry. Is your heart rate up? Are you shallow breathing? Do your joints hurt? Are there tears in your eyes? Do you want to hit someone? Are you yelling at someone or something? Are your muscles tense? Is your jaw clenched?

Step 3

Assess your body afterwards. Step back from yourself and feel how your body feels after the anger subsides. Become an observer of all your body and mind functions. Are you ashamed? Is your heart racing? Is your jaw tight? Is your stomach tight? Do your hands hurt from clenching your fists? Have you actually hurt someone either physically or mentally? How do they look? How does that make you feel? Do you feel really good or really bad? Did getting angry make you feel high or exhilarated?

Step 4

Recognize when it is about to happen. Observe when you first start to feel the anger rising up. Why are you becoming angry? What happened to start the process? Did someone hurt your feelings? Is your ego telling you that you are being put down or mistreated? Do you think you're being denigrated? Do you feel like you're acting like your father, mother, or whoever treated you this way? Do you really want to carry this through? What will you get out of becoming angry? How does your body feel? Is your body out of balance? Is that what's making this happen? Is your mind out of control? Does it feel like a train coming down the tracks? That it started by itself and you can't stop it? Is the reward for anger a burst of adrenaline that you need to make you feel high or superior to others?

If you notice that anger makes you feel really good, you will want to assess your lifestyle and make the dietary changes immediately. You might also need to see your doctor for a check-up. You might have a thyroid problem in addition to low blood sugar or yeast problems, as discussed in Chapters 2, 5, and 6. Ask your doctor to do a T3, T4, and TSH test to determine if you have hypothyroidism. This could explain why you become angry: to give yourself a burst of needed energy that you should be getting from your thyroid gland. You might also be low in many hormones, so doing a complete hormone panel is a good idea as well.

Step 5

Stop an anger attack before it starts. Once you have finished the first four steps and changed your diet and lifestyle, you will be able to stop an anger attack before it starts. It might even help to do what your grandmother said: stop and count to ten before you act. And then take slow, deep breaths. Change the subject if you need to change your mind. How does that feel? Do you feel in control of yourself? Are you happy to not react with anger in that situation? Have you avoided the racing heart, shallow breathing, and adrenaline rush? Are you calm, relaxed, and making appropriate comments instead of lashing out in anger?

Once you have discovered what triggers your anger, you can deal with that in a rational way. Work with a counselor, spiritual advisor, or person trained in helping others deal with strong emotions. You might even look for a chapter of Emotions Anonymous. You can also use the following anger-release exercises.

ANGER-RELEASE EXERCISE

Sit in a comfortable straight-backed chair with your feet flat on the floor and the small of your back pressed against the back of the chair. Put your hands on your thighs with the palms open, facing up in a relaxed position. Your chin should be parallel to the floor, lips together/teeth apart, tongue on the floor of your mouth in a relaxed position. Relax your shoulders by consciously making them drop and relax.

Starting at your waist and lower ribs, begin expanding and breathing in. Continue to inhale into the middle of your chest and then the upper part, using a count of five or six. Slowly exhale from the lower ribs and waist by raising the diaphragm up, up, and up until it reaches the top of the chest cavity and the lower ribs are contracted. Use the count of five or six to exhale.

Sit like this, relaxing and deep breathing, for a few minutes. Feel yourself relaxing more and more like you are sinking into the chair and then the floor as you relax. Let relaxation wash over you like a soft, refreshing mist. As the mist falls over you, continue to relax, sinking down and down, releasing the tension in each part of your body, starting at the head and traveling down until your feet are relaxed. Consciously relax each part by saying to yourself, "head relax," then let it relax, "neck relax," let it relax, "shoulders relax," and so on. Keep doing the slow, deep breathing to help with the relaxation. With each exhalation, let yourself relax more and more.

Once you are relaxed, imagine a scene in which you were happy and peaceful like sitting at the edge of a pond, under a tree in the park, or swinging on a swing in a playground. Let yourself feel how peaceful and happy you are for a minute or two. Continue the slow, deep breathing.

Let your mind drift to a time when you felt angry. Continue slow, deep breathing; keep relaxed. Allow your body and mind to feel relaxed and peaceful while reviewing the incident in your mind's eye. Let your peaceful demeanor defuse your angry feelings in this situation.

Drift back to the peaceful scene again and rest there for a few more minutes while slowly deep breathing. Let this feeling of being relaxed and peaceful flood your mind and body.

Each time you begin to feel angry, remember this exercise and recreate the peaceful, relaxed feeling again in your mind and body so that it begins to take the place of the angry feelings. Practice makes perfect, so it is said. The more you practice relaxing, being relaxed, and defusing the anger, the easier it will get. Eventually, you will be able to reduce your anger using the Anger Cure diet and supplements, as well as this relaxation technique.

FORGIVENESS ANGER-RELEASE TECHNIQUE

Follow the same relaxation and deep-breathing exercise described above. Once you are fully relaxed, imagine a scene in which you were happy and peaceful, and let yourself feel how peaceful and happy you are for a minute or two. Continue the slow, deep breathing; keep relaxing.

Let your mind drift to a time when you felt angry. Bring the scene to the front of your mind and watch the scene like it is a movie. Then begin the forgiveness exercise. Say out loud, "I forgive you and I forgive myself." You can embellish this by saying what you forgive the person or event for, such as, "I forgive you for tripping me in the elevator." Take a few slow, deep breaths. Then say, "And I forgive myself for being upset and getting angry." Do a few more slow, deep breaths. Then say, "I release the anger associated with this situation." Take a few more slow, deep breaths as you allow your body and mind to release the situation.

This technique can help you release the anger stored in your muscles, mind, and heart. Every day you can forgive someone. Say the words even if you don't feel them in your heart. Practice forgiving and you will soon begin to feel it. Don't hold on to something that is keeping you from total, vibrant health.

GUIDED TECHNIQUE

It is possible to do these techniques on your own and be successful, or you may want to use a recorded session. For that I recommend purchasing an anger-management CD. The ones I like can be ordered from the website of Dr. Eke Wokocha, a clinical psychologist in California. (You can order them from either www.alafiawellness.com or www.angercure.com.) His voice is very soothing, and the technique is very simple and easy to do.

I remember hearing from Katherine Kuhlman, a popular healer in the last century, that she found that many people she visited in the hospital with stomach cancer were holding on to some kind of resentment against a person, some as far back as fifty years. When they forgave the person, the stomach cancer cleared up. It can be that simple. Anger can kill you quickly or slowly.

"I can't seem to give up smoking. Can you help me?" a neighbor asked me one day.

"Sure," I said. So we did a relaxation exercise, and when he was relaxed, I asked him why he thought he couldn't give up smoking even though he had tried patches, hypnosis, and several other programs.

"I think it was what my father said to me when I was about ten and I had started smoking. He turned to me and said, 'Son, I know you're smoking and you better quit before you get into it any more because once you get older you won't be able to quit.' So now I'm older and I can't quit."

So we did the forgiveness exercise, and he forgave his father for saying that to him, and he forgave himself for believing it and holding on to the idea for twenty years. After he did the deep breathing and then released it, he was actually free of the desire to smoke. It was that simple for him.

THE POWER OF THE BODY/MIND CONNECTION

It's easy to see that the body/mind connection is very powerful. Once you follow the Anger Cure program for your body and mind, and can relax and be in control of yourself, your mind will be able to tell your body ways to reduce your anger. Both the diet and the relaxation techniques take time to perfect. Don't be harsh on yourself; just practice both until you no longer have anger.

How Long Will It Take?

How long it takes depends on you. How long have you had the problem? One week, one year, ten years, forty years? The longer you have had the habit, the longer it may take to change it. You notice I say "may" here because if you follow the diet, take the supplements, and do the relaxation exercises, it may take you way less time than if you try other ways. Following the complete Anger Cure program will help your body and mind become healthy so that you are not controlled by habits or voices telling you to do something you know isn't right. Take charge of your body and mind so that you are the one running your life.

Adult Behavior

Please don't let a habit, nutritional deficiency, poor lifestyle choices, or the fight-or-flight syndrome run your body and mind. As an adult you have the choice to make changes in your life. If anger and angry outbursts are running your life, you can change. You can feel better about yourself.

Don't let a decision you made as a child rule your life as an adult. Forgive the person and yourself, release the situation and the anger associated with it, and be free. Follow the Anger Cure program fully and soon you will have no anger problem.

WHAT IF IT DOESN'T WORK?

There are some exceptions that limit the success of the Anger Cure program. If you have liver damage that can't be repaired, if you are taking medication that actually causes the anger, if you have a disease or condition that is related to anger problems like Tourette's syndrome, you can use the Anger Cure program to get as healthy as possible and reduce the anger, but it may not be fully effective. Let your doctor know that you want to follow this diet and lifestyle plan, discuss it thoroughly, and then follow his or her advice. Do not stop taking any prescription drugs without the consent of your doctor.

CHAPTER SUMMARY

1. It is possible to change something about your body using your mind. This is called the body/mind connection.

2. It's easy to change a habit by following just five steps.

3. Try the simple body/mind forgiveness exercises for defusing anger and angry outbursts.

4. Many famous faith healers used the body/mind connection as a way of determining an illness and releasing it.

Notes

Chapter 1

1. S. Seshadri, A. Beiser, J. Selhub, et al., "Plasma homocysteine as a risk factor for dementia and Alzheimer's disease," *New England Journal of Medicine* (2002): 476–83.

2. L.J. Su, L. Arab, "Nutritional status of folate and colon cancer risk: evidence from NHANES I epidemiologic follow-up study," *Annals of Epidemiology* (2001): 11:65–72.

Chapter 2

1. K.B. Koh, C.H. Kim, J.K. Park, "Predominance of anger in depressive disorders compared with anxiety disorders and somatoform disorders," *Journal of Clinical Psychiatry* (June 2002): 486–92.

2. Adelle Davis, *Let's Eat Right to Keep Fit* (New York, NY: New American Library, 1970).

3. J.C. Brand-Miller, S.H. Holt, D.B. Pawlak, J. McMillan, "Glycemic index and obesity," *American Journal of Clinical Nutrition* (July 2002): 281S–5S.

Chapter 3

1. Anthony Cichoke, *The Complete Book of Enzyme Therapy* (Garden City Park, NY: Avery Publishing Group, 1999), p. 404.

Chapter 4

1. Anthony Cichoke, *The Complete Book of Enzyme Therapy* (Garden City Park, NY: Avery Publishing Group, 1999), p. 10.

2. Kathleen O'Bannon Baldinger, *The World's Oldest Health Plan* (Lancaster, PA: Starburst Publishers, 1994), p. 35.

3. James F. Balch and Phyllis A. Balch, *Prescription for Nutritional Healing,* 3rd ed. (New York, NY: Avery, 2000), p. 679.

4. *The American Journal of Medicine* (2005); 118: 778–81.

Chapter 5

1. Jack Challem, Burton Berkson, and Melissa Diane Smith, *Syndrome X: The Complete Nutritional Program to Prevent and Reverse Insulin Resistance* (New York, NY: John Wiley & Sons, 2000), p. 25.

2. Kathleen DesMaisons, *Potatoes Not Prozac* (New York, NY: Simon & Schuster, 1998), p. 68.

3. Challem, *Syndrome X,* p. 48.

4. N.M. McKeown, J.B. Meigs, S. Liu, et al., "Whole-grain intake is favorably associated with metabolic risk factors for type 2 diabetes and cardiovascular disease in the Framingham Offspring Study," *American Journal of Clinical Nutrition* (August 2002): 390–8.

5. Review, "Hypomagnesemia in acute and chronic illness," *Critical Care Nursing Quarterly* (August 2000): 1–19.

6. D. Ziegler et al., "Alpha-lipoic acid in the treatment of diabetic polyneuropathy in Germany: current evidence from clinical trials," *Experimental and Clinical Endocrinology and Diabetes* (1999): 421–30.

7. J. Welihinda et al. "Effect of *Momordica charantia* on the glucose tolerance in maturity onset diabetics," *Journal of Ethnopharmacology* (September 1986): 277–82.

8. A. Gupta, R. Gupta, B. Lal, "Effect of *Trigonella foenum-graecum* (fenugreek) seeds on glycaemic control and insulin resistance in type 2 diabetes mellitus: a double-blind placebo-controlled study," *Journal of the Associations of Physicians of India* (November 2001): 1057–61.

Chapter 6

1. William G. Crook, *The Yeast Connection: A Medical Breakthrough* (Jackson, TN: Professional Books, 1983).

2. Kathleen O'Bannon Baldinger, *The World's Oldest Health Plan* (Lancaster, PA: Starburst Publishers, 1994), pp. 124–130.

3. Jeanne Marie Martin, with Zoltan Rona, *Complete Candida Yeast Guidebook,* revised 2nd ed. (Roseville, CA: Prima Publishing, 2000), p. 196.

Chapter 7

1. J.M. Watson, M.J. Lunt, S. Morris, et al., "Reversal of caffeine withdrawal by ingestion of a soft beverage," *Pharmacology Biochemistry and Behavior* (May 2000); 66(1): 15-8.

Chapter 8

1. H. Hurt, E. Malmud, N.L. Brodsky, J. Giannetta, "Exposure to violence: psychological and academic correlates in child witnesses," *Archives of Pediatric and Adolescent Medicine* (December 2001): 1351-6.

2. B. Pfefferbaum, S.J. Nixon, R.D. Tivis, et al., "Television exposure in children after a terrorist incident," *Psychiatry* (Fall 2001): 202-11.

3. M.A. Schuster, B.D. Stein, L. Jaycox, et al., "A national survey of stress reactions after the September 11, 2001, terrorist attacks," *New England Journal of Medicine* (November 2001): 1507-12.

4. J.G. Johnson, P. Cohen, E.M. Smailes, et al., "Television viewing and aggressive behavior during adolescence and adulthood," *Science* (March 2002): 2468-71.

5. M.V. Singer, "Effect of ethanol and alcoholic beverages on the gastrointestinal tract in humans," *Romanian Journal of Gastroenterology* (September 2002): 197-204.

6. D.P. Phillips, G.C. Liu, K. Kwok, et al., "The Hound of the Baskervilles effect: natural experiment on the influence of psychological stress on timing of death," *British Medical Journal* (December 2001): 1443-67.

7. M. Kivimaki, P. Leino-Arjas, R. Luukkonen, et al., "Work stress and risk of cardiovascular mortality: prospective cohort study of industrial employees," *British Medical Journal* (October 2002): 857-60.

8. M. Ritsner, R. Maayan, A. Gibel, et al., "Elevation of the cortisol/dehydroepiandrosterone ratio in schizophrenic patients," *European Neuropsychopharmacology* (August 2004); 14(4): 267-73.

Chapter 9

1. Patricia Hall Black and Ruth Little Carey, *Vegetarian Cookery,* vol. 5 (Mountain View, CA: Pacific Press Publishing Association, 1971).

2. Y.S. Diniz, A.A. Fernandes, K.E. Campos, et al., "Toxicity of hypercaloric diet and monosodium glutamate: oxidative stress and metabolic shifting in hepatic tissue," *Food Chemistry Toxocology* (February 2004); 42(2): 313–19.

APPENDIX A

The Importance of B Vitamins

The official measurement of how much of each nutrient you need in a day is called the RDA, which stands for recommended dietary allowance or recommended daily allowance. Generally, this amount is just enough to keep a person alive, and in some cases not even that. This appendix will tell you what the RDA is and what holistic practitioners feel you need. I call this the HA, or holistic allowance. Also listed are the best food sources for each B vitamin.

B VITAMINS

All the B complex vitamins are water soluble. That means that water breaks them down or rinses them out of your body. For this reason they must be taken frequently over the day whether in food or supplement form. They are also heat and light soluble so all the foods and supplements containing B vitamins should be kept in a cool, dark place or package. Many times people who work out to the point of perspiring need more B vitamins because the heat and water in their bodies remove or use up the B vitamins. Always take B vitamins in combination with the entire B complex, and take them three or four times a day in low doses such as 12–25 milligrams (mg) each of the major Bs.

Vitamin B$_1$ (thiamine)

Vitamin B$_1$ plays an essential role in the metabolism of carbohydrates. A deficiency is first seen in nerve and brain function. Beriberi is the name given to the classic symptoms of thiamine deficiency. This is very rare in modern times.

RDA: 1.1 mg for women; 1.5 mg for men

HA: 25–300 mg for women and men

Best food sources: whole grains, organ meats like liver, pork, soybeans, egg yolks, oatmeal, poultry, and fish

Vitamin B$_2$ (riboflavin)

Vitamin B$_2$ is important for the metabolism of proteins, fats, and carbohydrates. It is often called the youth vitamin because it is essential for healthy hair and skin and for disease resistance. Deficiency symptoms include an inability to adjust to bright lights, oily skin and hair, shredding of the lips, and paper cuts at the corners of the mouth, nose, or eyes.

RDA: 1.3 mg for women; 1.7 mg for men

HA: 25–300 mg for women and men

Best food sources: milk, cheese, yogurt, organ meats, eggs, avocados, asparagus, broccoli, liver, kidney, and nuts

Vitamin B$_3$ (niacin or niacinamide)

Often called the "courage" vitamin because of its extensive use in the 1970s for schizophrenia, vitamin B$_3$ is used to help lower cholesterol, triglycerides, and VLDL (very-low-density lipoprotein), and is most effective when used in combination with chromium.

RDA: 15 mg for women; 19 mg for men

HA: 25–300 mg for women and men

Best food sources: beef, pork, fish, milk and cheese, eggs, potatoes, broccoli, carrots, liver, green vegetables, and beans

Vitamin B$_5$ (pantothenic acid or calcium pantothenate)

Vitamin B$_5$ often called the antistress vitamin because it is essential for the healthy functioning of the adrenal glands and immune system. Make sure you have enough of this vitamin if you are under any stress at all. It is also important for the metabolism of fats, carbohydrates, and proteins and has been known to remove "age spots" from the skin.

RDA: none

HA: 25–300 mg for women and men

Best food sources: egg yolks, dairy products, potatoes, peas, beans, whole-wheat berries, orange juice, pork, beef, liver, saltwater fish, and salmon

Vitamin B$_6$ (pyridoxine)

Vitamin B$_6$ is the most widely used and needed of the B vitamins. It is essential for the health of the skin and nervous system; necessary for the production of serotonin and other neurotransmitters in the brain; useful for carpal tunnel syndrome, PMS (premenstrual syndrome), and when taking oral or patch contraceptives to eliminate the side effects of water retention; useful in reversing "pregnancy mask" or dark discoloration around the edges of the face in women on birth control pills, under stress, or during pregnancy. Pyridoxine should be taken with vitamin B$_2$ and zinc.

RDA: 1.2 mg for women; 2.0 mg for men

HA: 25–300 mg for women and men

Best food sources: eggs, fish (especially herring and salmon), spinach, carrots, chicken, walnuts, sunflower seeds, cabbage, peanuts, and brewer's yeast

Vitamin B$_{12}$ (cobalamin)

Vitamin B$_{12}$ is essential for fat and carbohydrate metabolism and is often given to the elderly to help with memory and dementia. It is generally found only in animal products, so it is often deficient in végans or people who do not eat any animal products and in people with compromised digestive systems, like the elderly. (Tempeh, a fermented soybean product is the only major source of B_{12} for strict vegetarians.)

RDA: 2 micrograms (mcg) for women and men

HA: 25–300 mcg for women and men

Best food sources: all animal proteins; highest sources: 3 ounces of liver contains 95 mcg, $\frac{1}{4}$ cup of chicken livers contains 6.7 mcg, 3 ounces of rainbow trout contains 5.36 mcg, $\frac{3}{4}$ cup of tempeh contains 1 mcg, $\frac{2}{3}$ cup of plain yogurt (with active culture) contains 1 mcg

Folic Acid, Folate, or Folacin (formerly called vitamin B_9)

This vitamin works closely with B_6 and B_{12} in preventing elevated levels of homocysteine shown to be involved with heart problems. It is essential for the production of RNA and DNA and useful for preventing birth defects, including neural tube defects.

RDA: 180 mcg for women; 200 mcg for men

HA: 400–1,200 mcg for women and men

Best food sources: dark green leafy vegetables (including kale, mustard, beet, and turnip greens), spinach, black beans, kidney beans, peanut butter, soybeans, cottage cheese, eggs, avocados, blackberries, beef, lamb, pork, chicken livers, asparagus, broccoli, liver, and kidneys

Biotin

Biotin, while not officially a vitamin, is classified as part of the B vitamin complex. It is involved in the metabolism of carbohydrates and used in the synthesis of proteins and fats. Eating raw egg whites frequently can cause a biotin deficiency.

RDA: none

HA: 30–100 mcg for women and men

Best food sources: lamb, chicken, pork, beef, veal, liver, nutritional yeasts, milk, cheeses, saltwater fish, whole-wheat products, rice bran, and algae like chlorella and spirulina

Choline, Inositol, and PABA (para-aminobenzoic acid)

Choline, inositol, and PABA are considered part of the B complex, but are not true vitamins. They are essential for the metabolism of fats, phospholipids, and fatty acids. Choline is made into acetylcholine, which has long been used to restore brain function in people who have had accidents and experience memory loss or inability to think clearly. It is critical for nerve function. Inositol is useful in the metabolism of fat. PABA aids bacteria in the formation of folic acid in the body. PABA, as an ingredient in cosmetics, can function as a sunblock. PABA film or cream has been used topically to restore hair color, along with good B complex vitamins, zinc, and copper taken orally.

RDA: none

HA: 25–200 mg for women and men

Best food sources: *choline*–egg yolks, brain, heart, dark green leafy vegetables, legumes, liver, and wheat germ; *inositol*–nuts, whole grains, milk, meats, yeast, and fruits; *PABA*–dark green leafy vegetables, organ meats, yogurt, wheat germ, and brewer's yeast

APPENDIX B

Selected Recipes

These recipes are easy to do and taste great. I have kept them simple so you will want to try them and use them frequently with your new Anger Cure lifestyle.

Black Bean Tofu Dip

$1/4$ onion, chopped fine
$1/2$ clove garlic, chopped fine
1 teaspoon olive oil
2 cups cooked, rinsed, and drained black beans
$1/2$ cup drained tofu
$1/2$ teaspoon chili powder
1 teaspoon ground cumin
$1/4$ teaspoon ground tarragon
2 teaspoons balsamic or tarragon vinegar

Sauté onion and garlic in the olive oil until golden. Put all ingredients in food processor and process to desired consistency. Use for dipping vegetables. Serves 4–6.

Creamed Chicken Soup

Base

4 whole cloves

3 cloves garlic

1 onion, whole, unpeeled, but washed

$\frac{1}{2}$ lemon

1 5–6 pound natural roasting chicken, cut in pieces or whole

2 carrots, unpeeled

3 stalks celery, halved

6 black peppercorns

2 bay leaves

4 sprigs fresh parsley

Water to cover

Soup

2 tablespoons chicken fat from base, or butter

1 onion, peeled and chopped

1 clove garlic, chopped

2 carrots, chopped

3 stalks celery, chopped

3 turnips, cubed

3 tablespoons arrowroot starch

1 package frozen cut green beans

1 bunch fresh spinach or package of frozen chopped spinach

1. To make the base: Stick the cloves into the onion. Wash the lemon and thinly slice it. Place all ingredients in a large stock or soup pot. Turn heat to medium and bring it just to simmer. Don't let it boil or it will make a gray scum on top and the base won't be as nice. You can do this in a slow cooker if you want. Cook until the meat starts to fall off the bones. It may take two or more hours. The slower you can cook this, the better the stock will be.

Remove the chicken and put in the refrigerator. Strain the stock into a large bowl to remove the herbs and seasonings. Press the veggies to get the flavor out. Refrigerate stock overnight. Remove the fat and save it for other uses.

2. To make the soup: Put 2 tablespoons of the fat from the stock into a clean soup pot. Heat over medium heat. Add onion, garlic, carrots, and celery and cook until

slightly brown. Remove the meat from the chicken bones and shred it. Add the turnips and half of the chicken stock to the pot and cook over medium heat until turnips are soft. Remove turnips. Add the chicken and continue to heat. Dissolve the arrowroot starch in a cup of cool broth. Blend or purée the cooked turnips with the arrowroot mixture. Add to the simmering soup. When it begins to thicken, add the chicken and remaining veggies. Heat through. Add remaining stock as needed. This makes a lot of soup, perfect for a party or large family. Store some in serving-sized containers in the freezer for later use as snacks or meals. Serves 8–12 or more.

Cabbage Salad Meal

Cream Dressing

$\frac{1}{4}$ *cup unsweetened yogurt*

$\frac{1}{4}$ *cup sour cream*

2 tablespoons lemon juice

$\frac{1}{4}$ *teaspoon finely grated lemon peel*

$\frac{1}{2}$ *teaspoon Dijon mustard*

1 teaspoon sea salt

1 teaspoon xylitol

$\frac{1}{2}$ *teaspoon ground coriander seeds*

Salad

1 cup shredded precooked meat or tuna

2 cups shredded cabbage

1 small carrot, grated

3 sprigs fresh parsley, dill, or cilantro, finely chopped

$\frac{1}{4}$ *sweet onion, chopped, OR 2 green onions, chopped*

1 small zucchini, grated

$\frac{1}{2}$ *cup toasted and chopped whole almonds*

1. To make the dressing, beat all ingredients together and chill before serving.

2. To toast the almonds for the salad, spread them in a dry pan over medium-low heat. Shake the pan frequently to prevent burning and flip the almonds to toast both sides. Cool before slicing or chopping.

3. To make the salad, mix all ingredients together and moisten with cream dressing. Serve on a bed of lettuce. Serves 2.

Cream Cheese and Sprout Balls

*1 package commercial cream cheese, softened,
or homemade yogurt cheese
(see Yogurt Cheese recipe on page 213)*

*$\frac{1}{2}$ cup chopped sprouts
(such as alfalfa, radish, fenugreek, or mung bean)*

$\frac{1}{4}$ cup chopped sunflower and pumpkin seeds

*2 sprigs fresh herbs (such as basil, mint, cilantro, thyme, or chives),
chopped fine*

Mash the cream cheese until soft or use a mixer, electric beaters, or food processor. Try not to add any additional liquid. Stir in the remaining ingredients and form into balls. Leave in the refrigerator overnight on a plate with no cover on it, so that the balls dry out a little. Wrap in plastic wrap or put in little snack-size bags. Keep refrigerated until eaten. Serves 4–6.

Egg Foo Yung

2 green onions

4 mushrooms, if allowed

$\frac{1}{4}$ red or green pepper

1–3 teaspoons oil or butter for cooking

2 eggs

2 teaspoons cold water

1 teaspoon tamari soy sauce, if allowed

1 teaspoon arrowroot starch (optional)

1 cup mung bean sprouts

Cut onions, mushrooms, and pepper into matchstick-sized pieces. Heat oil over medium heat and sauté veggies until just slightly soft. Remove from heat and set aside. Beat eggs, water, tamari and arrowroot together, and mix in cooked veggies and raw sprouts. Heat pan over medium-high heat and brush with oil. Spoon egg/veggie mixture on it and cook until it is set on the top and then turn and finish cooking. It should take about five to seven minutes altogether. Serves 2–4.

Fried Brown Rice

2 teaspoons oil

1–2 drops toasted sesame oil

1 egg, beaten with 1 teaspoon water or milk

1/4 onion, chopped

1 clove garlic, chopped

1/2 inch piece of ginger, grated

1 small stem broccoli, separated and chopped

1/8 small red pepper, chopped

1/4 cup chopped cooked meat

1/2 cup precooked brown or brown basmati rice, chilled

1/4 cup chopped cilantro

Sprinkling soy sauce, if allowed

Heat 1 teaspoon of oil in pan over medium-high heat until hot. Pour in beaten egg and let cook until just firm. Remove from pan and put on paper towel. Add remaining oil to pan and, when hot, sauté onion, garlic, ginger, and broccoli stems. When onions turn transparent, add red peppers, meat, and broccoli florets. Stir frequently. Slice the egg into matchstick pieces. When broccoli stems turn bright green, reduce the heat to low and add the rice, egg, and cilantro and stir. If you don't have a yeast problem you can add a sprinkling of soy sauce near the end. Serve hot. Serves 1.

Note: You can use any combination of veggies, either fresh or precooked. You can even add frozen stir-fry mixed veggies, just make sure they are heated thoroughly.

High-Protein Macaroni and Cheese with Veggies

1 ½ cups water, vegetable cooking water, or tomato juice

1 teaspoon sea salt

1 cup whole wheat, spelt, or high-protein macaroni

2 cups chopped mixed vegetables (such as onion, garlic, mushrooms, carrot, celery, broccoli, green beans, red or green peppers)

¼ cup milk powder

½ cup milk

1 ½ cups shredded or cubed cheddar cheese

2 tablespoons sesame seeds

Bring water to a boil and add salt. Add macaroni slowly so that water continues to boil. Stir to keep from sticking. (If it seems to be sticking, add 1 teaspoon of oil to the water.) While cooking, add veggies starting with the hardest first, like carrots, and ending with any leaves or herbs. Cook for a total of ten minutes. After ten minutes is up, remove from heat, add milk powder, milk, and 1 cup of the cheese and blend together. Spoon into casserole dish and top with remaining cheese and sesame seeds. Bake in preheated 325°F oven for twenty minutes.

Try to use high-protein pasta and low-glycemic veggies for this dish. Serves 4.

Variation: This dish is also nice when tomatoes, green peppers, garlic, onions, mushrooms, and 1 teaspoon each of basil and oregano are used.

Italian Tomato and Mozzarella Salad

6 leaves fresh basil OR 2 teaspoon dried basil

1 clove garlic

4 tablespoons fresh lemon juice or balsamic vinegar

2 tablespoons extra-virgin olive oil

Salt and pepper to taste

1 ripe tomato

6 slices of mozzarella, either presliced or sliced from the ball

Make a neat pile of the basil leaves on a cutting board. Roll them up like a jelly roll from the long side so you have a long tube of basil leaves, kind of like a green cigar. Carefully slice the roll of leaves into very thin shreds of basil. (If you are using dried basil, crumble them between your fingers into the lemon juice or vinegar.) Press garlic in a garlic press into the vinegar or lemon juice, add olive oil, salt, and pepper, and mix with a fork. Set dressing aside.

Slice tomato into 6 slices. Using a large plate, alternate layering the tomatoes with the cheese, and place the basil shreds on top of each tomato slice. Make a circular pattern around the plate. Drizzle the dressing over it. Serves 1–2.

Jamaican Black Bean Soup

This is great to take with you in an insulated bottle for lunch or snacks.

3 tablespoons extra-virgin olive oil or butter, or a mixture

1 large sweet onion, chopped

2 ribs celery, chopped

3 cloves fresh garlic, pressed or chopped

1 tablespoon oat flour

6 cups cold water or stock

3 cups cooked black beans (2 15-ounce cans)

$1/4$ cup chopped parsley

2 teaspoons natural liquid smoke

2 bay leaves

2 teaspoons ground cumin

$1/2$ cup nonalcoholic sherry or other dry sherry

3 tablespoon white wine or Balsamic vinegar

Salt and pepper to taste

1 cup sour cream or yogurt for serving

Heat large soup pot over medium heat and add oil or butter. Sauté onion, celery, and garlic until onion is translucent. Sprinkle flour over the veggies and stir to coat. Cook one minute more to toast the flour. Add water and stir. Add black beans, parsley, liquid smoke, bay leaves, cumin, sherry, vinegar, and salt and pepper. Stir. Allow the food to come to just barely simmering, reduce heat to keep it simmering, and cook, covered, for one hour or more. Serve with a dollop of sour cream or yogurt. Serves 6–10.

Variation: Add leftover cooked meat just before serving. This is also fabulous with chopped shrimp added.

Lettuce Roll-Ups

Lettuce leaves (leaf, romaine, green iceberg, and so on)
Nut butter (peanut, almond, pistachio, sunflower seed, and so on)
Toothpicks

Wash and dry lettuce. Spread about 1 tablespoon of the nut butter on each leaf and roll up. Fasten with a toothpick to keep them closed.

Kids love this! If you use peanut butter, make sure it has no sugar or artificial ingredients. Serves as many as desired.

Meat and Vegetable Soup

1 tablespoon butter
1 tablespoon extra-virgin olive oil
1 onion, peeled and chopped fine
3 cloves fresh garlic, peeled and chopped fine
1 carrot, chopped fine
5 celery stalks, chopped medium
1 pound stew meat or ground beef
2 turnips, chopped in $\frac{1}{2}$ inch cubes
4 Roma tomatoes (plum tomatoes), chopped fine
$\frac{1}{2}$ cup red lentils
1 pound green beans cut in 1 inch pieces
3 sprigs fresh thyme, or 2 teaspoons dried thyme
1 teaspoon sea salt
Grinding of black pepper
Water

Heat a soup pot over medium-high heat and add the butter and oil. When butter is melted add the onion, garlic, carrot, and celery and stir. Cook until the onions just begin to change color, and add the meat and stir. Stir frequently. When the meat is browned add the turnips, tomatoes, and red lentils and stir. Cover with water and add 2 cups more water. Cover pot, turn heat to simmer, and cook for fifteen minutes. Remove cover and add green beans, thyme, salt, and black pepper. Add more water if needed. Cook until beans are tender and serve. Serves 4.

Variation—Meat and Vegetable Stew: Follow the instructions for Meat and Vegetable Soup, but add less water. Vegetables can be varied using the low-glycemic veggies listed in Chapter 5. Barley can be used instead of or in addition to lentils. Barley takes longer to cook and requires more water so adjust the recipe accordingly.

Variation—High-Protein Pasta Soup and Veggies: Make the Meat and Vegetable Soup but use high-protein pasta instead of lentils. High-protein pasta can be found in select grocery stores or health food stores.

Middle Eastern Cucumber Salad

1 regular cucumber or $\frac{1}{2}$ *English cucumber*

$\frac{1}{2}$ *cup yogurt*

2 teaspoons lemon juice

1 teaspoon ground cumin

1 can chickpeas, rinsed and drained

1 green onion, chopped

3 sprigs fresh mint, chopped

Peel regular cucumber, cut it in half lengthwise, and slice. Remove seeds if they are tough. If using English cucumber, don't peel or remove seeds. Mix yogurt, lemon juice, and cumin together. Add remaining ingredients and mix well. Refrigerate to blend the flavors. Serves 4 as an appetizer.

Mushroom* and Barley Soup

$\frac{1}{2}$ pound mushrooms

3 tablespoons vegetable oil

$\frac{1}{3}$ cup pot barley

6 cups boiling water or stock

1 stalk celery

3 sprigs fresh parsley

1 teaspoon sea salt

Do not eat mushrooms if you have a yeast problem.

Remove stems from mushrooms and chop; slice the caps. Heat oil in a soup pot over medium heat. Sauté caps for two minutes or until they change color and remove pan from heat. Remove mushroom caps and set aside. Add the barley to the oil, stir, and sauté until it turns golden; add the chopped mushroom stems and stir and sauté one minute more. Add the remaining ingredients, except the caps, and boil hard for three minutes. Then simmer for twenty to thirty minutes more until barley is soft and cooked through. Remove celery and parsley and dispose of them, add the caps, and simmer for three or four minutes more to heat caps. Serves 4.

My Mother's Cucumber Salad

1 regular cucumber

$\frac{1}{2}$ small, sweet onion

1 cup vinegar

2 teaspoons xylitol

Peel cucumber and cut in half lengthwise. Slice into thin crescents. Peel onion and slice into thin crescents. Mix vinegar and xylitol together in nonaluminum pan, and heat until almost boiling. Pour over the cucumbers and onions and chill for several hours. Serves 4 as a side salad.

Oat Bran Muffins

3 tablespoons melted butter

1 egg

1 cup milk

$\frac{1}{4}$ cup oat bran

$\frac{1}{4}$ cup sunflower or pumpkin seeds, walnuts, or pecans

2 cups whole-oat flour

1 teaspoon ground cinnamon

1 teaspoon baking powder

3 tablespoons xylitol

Preheat oven to 400°F. Place butter, egg, milk, oat bran, and seeds/nuts in a food processor fitted with a plastic blade. Process until egg is well beaten. Sift in remaining ingredients, using a sifter, and pulse several times to moisten all the ingredients. Do not overmix or muffins will be heavy. Mixture should be lumpy. Fill ten to twelve papered muffin tins $\frac{3}{4}$ full. Bake for twenty to thirty minutes or until toothpick inserted in the middle comes out clean. Refrigerate after the muffins are cool.

Oatmeal with Broccoli, Ginger, Garlic, and Olive Oil or Butter

Oatmeal (not instant)

$\frac{1}{4}$ cup chopped broccoli

$\frac{1}{4}$ teaspoon grated fresh ginger

$\frac{1}{4}$ clove fresh garlic, finely chopped or pressed

1 teaspoon butter or olive oil

Cook oatmeal according to directions on package. Add in $\frac{1}{4}$ cup chopped broccoli and $\frac{1}{4}$ teaspoon grated fresh ginger for each serving while oatmeal is cooking. Add finely chopped or pressed fresh garlic to the bowl with a teaspoon of butter or olive oil, and serve oatmeal on it. Stir. Serves 1.

Use at least $\frac{1}{4}$ of a clove of garlic for each serving. You can add more, it just depends on your day and if you are meeting people. Generally, garlic only smells bad if you heat it up with the food, which is why I suggest adding it after the oatmeal is cooked.

Oven-Roasted Veggies

Pure olive oil spray or 2 tablespoons olive oil

2 pounds pearl onions or shallots, peeled (cut shallots in quarters)

1 pound zucchini, cut in thick 1 inch strips

2 large red or yellow bell peppers, seeded and cut in eighths

4 Brussels sprouts, quartered

2 stalks celery cut in 1 inch pieces

2 sprigs fresh basil, rosemary, or thyme, finely chopped

Preheat oven to 400°F. Spray veggies with oil or toss to coat if not using spray. Place the veggies on a cookie sheet in a single layer. Bake in the oven for twenty-five to thirty-five minutes or until browned and soft. Serves 4–6.

Any combination of veggies can be used for this. If you are having protein and a salad, you may even want to use a few quartered new potatoes in with the other veggies.

Protein Shake

$1/2$ piece of low-glycemic fruit if desired

1 cup soy or dairy milk, organic if possible

$1/4$–$1/2$ cup tofu*

$1/2$ cup fresh sprouts, such as alfalfa or mung bean

*Please make sure that the tofu you use is labeled either non-GMO (non-genetically modified organism) or organically grown.

Put all ingredients in a blender and blend until smooth. Drink. You can also add a green powder supplement made from wheat grass, barley grass, and/or spirulina for additional nutrients. Serves 1.

Salade Niçoise

Dressing

2 tablespoons extra-virgin olive oil

4 tablespoons lemon juice

1 clove garlic, minced or pressed

1 teaspoon fresh tarragon, finely chopped OR $\frac{1}{2}$ teaspoon dried tarragon

Salad

Romaine lettuce

4–6 black olives, niçoise, Greek, or Italian

1 hard-boiled egg, cut in quarters

4 green beans, steamed to partially cook them

$\frac{1}{2}$ can tuna, drained

1 small new potato, steamed or boiled and cut in 8 pieces

1. To make the dressing, whisk oil, lemon juice, garlic, and tarragon together. Set aside.

2. To make the salad, cut lettuce into bite-sized pieces and put in a bowl, and add remaining ingredients.

3. Drizzle the dressing over the salad and serve. Serves 1.

Scrambled Tofu

2 teaspoons oil

1–3 drops toasted sesame oil

$\frac{1}{4}$ onion, chopped

1 clove garlic, chopped

$\frac{1}{2}$ inch piece of ginger, grated

1 small stem broccoli, separated and chopped

$\frac{1}{8}$ small red pepper, chopped

1 cup well-drained, mashed firm tofu*

$\frac{1}{4}$ teaspoon turmeric, optional for color

$\frac{1}{4}$ cup chopped cilantro, parsley, basil, or other herbs

*To drain the tofu, I use several layers of towels under and over tofu and then place a cutting board or flat plate on top to gently press the water out. A small jar of water with a tight-fitting lid can be placed on the top as a weight to help press out water. (Please make sure that the tofu you use is labeled either non-GMO or organically grown.)

Heat oils in pan over medium-high heat. When hot add the onion, garlic, ginger, and broccoli stems. Stir. When the stems turn bright green, add the peppers and stir. Add the broccoli florets. Mash tofu with turmeric and continue to drain. Reduce the heat to low and add the tofu and chopped herbs. Stir and heat. Use a paper towel to soak up any water that seeps out of the tofu while heating. Serves 1.

Note: Any combination of veggies can be used for this recipe. Even frozen stir-fry mixed veggies can be used, just make sure they are heated thoroughly.

Steamed Veggies and Boiled Egg

1 very small potato with the skin on, cut into 6 pieces
$\frac{1}{8}$ sweet potato, cut into pieces like potato
1 small piece of broccoli, separated and stem chopped
2 green beans
$\frac{1}{4}$ cup chopped cabbage, kale, or collards
1 or 2 eggs, room temperature
Butter or olive oil to taste
Salt and pepper to taste

Heat steamer to boiling. Add the potatoes and broccoli stems and set the timer for five minutes. When it rings add the green beans, cabbage, broccoli tops, and whole eggs. Set the timer for another four or five minutes. Remove veggies from the steamer to the bowl, and put the eggs in cold water to stop the cooking and make them manageable for serving. Add butter or olive oil and salt and pepper to taste to the veggies. Using the blade of a table knife crack each eggshell around, open it into two halves, and scoop the egg onto the veggies. Serves 1.

Note: If you use cold eggs the steam will make them crack, so I generally soak them in hot water for a few minutes to warm them up.

Stir-Fried Chicken Livers with Red and Green Peppers, Onions, Garlic, and Ginger

1 tablespoon butter or olive oil

$\frac{1}{4}$ small onion or $\frac{1}{16}$ sweet onion, cut in thin strips

$\frac{1}{8}$ sweet red pepper, cut in thin strips

$\frac{1}{8}$ green pepper, cut in thin strips

2 whole chicken livers, cut in 4 or 6 pieces each

1 clove fresh garlic, chopped

$\frac{1}{2}$ inch fresh ginger, peeled and grated

Heat butter or oil in heavy fry pan and prepare veggies and livers while butter melts. Do not let butter burn. Put onion strips in the pan and stir, cook for a few seconds, then add the pepper strips and stir. Cook for about ten seconds, add the livers, garlic, and ginger, and stir. Cook until livers are just pink. Serves 1 as is, or more when served with saifun. (Saifun, bean thread noodles, are available in most Oriental grocery stores, supermarkets, or health food stores).

Stuffed Avocado

2 avocados

4–6 leaves of leaf lettuce

Slice of fresh lemon

4 small cooked shrimp, chopped fine

$\frac{1}{4}$ cup finely chopped sunflower seeds

1 rib celery, chopped fine

1 green onion, chopped fine

1 cup medium-chopped sprouts with green leaves

$\frac{1}{4}$ cup finely chopped fresh cilantro or mint

Mayonnaise to moisten

Wash avocados and dry well. Spread the leaf lettuce on two plates with the ribs in the center of the plate. Slice the avocados in half lengthwise, remove the pit, and rub the cut side of the avocado with the fresh lemon slice to keep it from turning dark. Put two halves on each plate. Trim the bottom of the avocado to make it lie flat if it is not sitting still. Mix remaining ingredients together and fill the hollows in the avocados, allowing some of the filling to drape artistically over one side if there is more than enough to fill the hollows. Serve immediately. Serves 2 as a main dish. Can serve 4 as a snack or appetizer if you put each half on a small plate with lettuce.

Stuffed Celery Sticks

Celery

Cream cheese with herbs

Nut butter

Wash and dry celery sticks. Cut off the fat white end if you want to. Use the greenest celery you can find. Cut into uniform lengths. Fill the center with cream cheese or nut butter. Make as many as you need for a snack or appetizer.

Stuffed Peppers

6 medium or 4 large sweet bell peppers, red, green, or yellow

1 tablespoon extra-virgin olive oil

$\frac{1}{2}$ onion, chopped

3–4 cloves fresh garlic, chopped

2 pounds ground meat, beef, veal, lamb, pork, chicken, or other meat

Grinding of black pepper to taste

3 large eggs

1 $\frac{1}{2}$ cups well-drained, mashed tofu*

2 tablespoons arrowroot starch

3 teaspoons ground cumin

1 tablespoon tamari soy sauce

1 $\frac{1}{2}$ tablespoons dried ground basil

1 $\frac{1}{2}$ tablespoons dried ground oregano

28-ounce can organic tomatoes in own juices

$\frac{1}{2}$ teaspoon cayenne pepper

*To drain the tofu, I use several layers of towels under and over tofu and then place a cutting board or flat plate on top to gently press the water out. A small jar of water with a tight-fitting lid can be placed on the top as a weight to help press out water. (Please make sure that the tofu you use is labeled either non-GMO or organically grown.)

Slice tops off peppers, remove seeds and veins, and discard. Trim the bottoms of the peppers to allow them to sit flat if needed. Heat olive oil in skillet or other large frying pan over medium heat. Chop onion and garlic coarsely and sauté in oil. Add meat when onion turns transparent. Stir and cook meat until no longer red. Cool and mix with black pepper, eggs, and tofu. Blend remaining ingredients in blender or food processor until smooth. Heat oven to 375°F. Fill peppers with the meat mixture, making the mixture level with the top of the pepper or a little under to allow for expansion, and place in nonmetal baking pan with a lid. Pour about 2 tablespoons of the tomato sauce into each pepper. Pour the remaining sauce into the dish surrounding the peppers. Cover and bake for one hour or more until the peppers are cooked and the filling set. Serve with the sauce spooned over the peppers. Serves 4–6.

This is a great meal to reheat. Many people like the peppers better the second day than freshly cooked.

Variation—Stuffed Cabbage Rolls: Substitute cabbage leaves for the peppers. Remove the thick vein and lightly steam the leaves so they can be rolled. Put the filling in and drizzle the sauce over before rolling the leaves. Start at the stem end and roll up, tucking in the sides in the first roll or so. Then pour the sauce over the tops and bake as above. It might take 8 to 12 large cabbage leaves, depending on the size of the leaves. I like to use Savoy cabbage for this recipe.

Tofu Salad

½ package extra-firm tofu

½ package soft tofu

6 green olives, sliced

1 stalk celery, chopped fine

½ teaspoon ground celery seeds

¼ teaspoon ground turmeric

Lettuce leaves

Fresh parsley, chopped, for garnish

Drain tofu in several layers of toweling to remove the excess liquid. I use several layers of towels under and over tofu and then place a cutting board or flat plate on top to gently press the water out. A small jar of water with a tight-fitting lid can be placed on the top as a weight to help press out water. Drain olives and wrap in paper towels to remove excess brine. Cube the extra-firm tofu into $1/4$- to $1/2$-inch pieces and put in a bowl with the celery, celery seeds, and olives. Mash the soft tofu with the turmeric. Mix both together. Serve on lettuce leaves and garnish with chopped fresh parsley. Serves 2.

Tuna Salad

1 can tuna, drained

1 stalk celery, chopped

2 tablespoons sweet onion, chopped OR 1 green onion, chopped

2–3 sprigs fresh parsley, finely chopped

6 green olives, rinsed, drained, and sliced or chopped

$1/4$ red or green pepper, chopped

2 hard-boiled eggs, chopped

Natural mayonnaise to moisten

Mix all ingredients together. You can serve the salad on a bed of leaf lettuce or put it on rice or oat crackers. This tuna salad can be served as a healthy sandwich if you use whole-grain sourdough bread and leaf or romaine lettuce. Serves 2.

Note: Having bread or sandwiches more than once a week is not recommended if you are dealing with severe anger and/or yeast problems.

Veggie Sticks with Guacamole Dip

1 ripe avocado

Juice of half a lemon or more

Cayenne pepper to taste

$1/2$ clove fresh garlic, pressed

$1/8$ onion, chopped

Mash or blend the avocado, adding enough lemon juice to make the desirable consistency. Stir in remaining ingredients to taste. Keep covered to prevent darkening. Serve with cut veggie sticks. Serves 2–4.

Variation: Add chopped tomatoes or chopped sweet red peppers to the dip.

Waldorf Salad Meal

2 apples (such as Jonathan, Jonagold, Spy), cored

2 stalks celery

$\frac{1}{2}$ cup walnut pieces

$\frac{1}{4}$ cup sunflower seeds

$\frac{1}{4}$ cup cubed cheddar cheese, if allowed*

$\frac{1}{4}$ cup mint or parsley, chopped finely

2 tablespoons chives, chopped finely

Natural mayonnaise to moisten

*Don't use the cheese if you have a yeast problem and/or are bothered by cheese.

Chop apples (skins on) and celery into even-sized pieces. Mix all ingredients together and serve on a bed of leaf or romaine lettuce. Serves 2 as a side salad.

Variation: Add chicken, or replace the cheese with chicken.

Yogurt Cheese

1 16-ounce container of natural yogurt,
full-fat or low-fat but not nonfat

Cheesecloth

Sieve, strainer, or colander

Put a double layer of cheesecloth in the sieve to line the bottom and sides. Pour the yogurt in and set over a bowl or pan in the refrigerator overnight or until the water (whey) is removed. Use in place of cream cheese. Makes about 1 cup.

Variation: Add salt, or fresh or dried herbs such as dill, basil, or marjoram.

Note: You can use the whey to water your plants—it will make them very green and nice.

HERBAL TEAS

For each of the following herbal teas, pour the specified amount of boiling water over the herbs in a teapot and let steep for at least five minutes. Strain and serve. Drink it all or share with a friend.

Relaxing Tea

1 teaspoon dried lavender flowers
1 teaspoon dried chamomile flowers
4 cups boiling water

Relaxing Tea for Children

1 teaspoon dried chamomile flowers
1 teaspoon dried catnip leaves
$\frac{1}{2}$ teaspoon dried mint leaves
4 cups boiling water
Honey (optional)

Calming Tea

1 teaspoon dried peppermint leaves
1 teaspoon dried lemon balm leaves
3 cups boiling water

Adrenal Helper Tea

2 teaspoons Fo-ti root (Ho Shou Wu)
1 teaspoon ginseng root
2 cups boiling water

Adrenal Helper Tea 2

1 teaspoon dried licorice root, chopped

$\frac{1}{2}$ teaspoon black cohosh root, chopped (optional)

$\frac{1}{2}$ teaspoon dried skullcap leaves

2 cups boiling water

Relaxing and Sleep-Inducing Tea

1 teaspoon dried lemon balm leaves

1 teaspoon dried passionflower flowers

$\frac{1}{2}$ teaspoon dried marjoram leaves

$\frac{1}{4}$–$\frac{1}{2}$ teaspoon dried valerian root

4 cups boiling water

Liver Helper Tea

1 teaspoon dandelion root

$\frac{1}{4}$ teaspoon burdock root

1 teaspoon globe artichoke leaves (Cynara scolymus)

$\frac{1}{2}$ teaspoon milk thistle seeds

1 teaspoon flaxseeds

2 teaspoons ground cinnamon

4 cups boiling water

Stomach Helper Tea

1 teaspoon fennel seeds

1 teaspoon dried chamomile flowers

1 teaspoon dried peppermint leaves

4 cups boiling water

Anger Cooling Tea

Inhale the relaxing aroma to calm anger, and drink.

3 teaspoons dried mint leaves

$\frac{1}{4}$ teaspoon chopped valerian root

1 teaspoon dried lemon balm leaves

4 cups boiling water

Honey (optional)

Suggested Reading

Allergies

Dumke, Nicolette. *Allergy Cooking with Ease.* Lancaster, PA: Starburst Publishers, 1992.

Katahn, Martin. *The Rotation Diet.* New York, NY: W.W. Norton & Company, 1986.

Mackarness, Richard. *Not All in the Mind: How Unsuspected Food Allergy Can Affect Your Body and Your Mind.* London and Sidney: Pan Books, 1979.

Rapp, Doris. *Allergies and Your Family.* New York, NY: Sterling Publishing Co., 1980.

———. *Allergies and the Hyperactive Child.* New York, NY: Cornerstone Library, 1979.

Anger and/or Rage

Potter-Efron, Ronald T. *Work Rage.* New York City, NY: Barnes & Noble Books, 1998.

Schauss, Alexander. *Diet, Crime, and Delinquency.* Berkeley, CA: Parker House, 1981.

Simontacchi, Carol. *The Crazy Makers: How the Food Industry Is Destroying Our Brains and Harming Our Children.* New York, NY: Jeremy Tarcher/Putnam, 2000.

Williams, Redford, and Virginia Williams. *Anger Kills.* New York City, NY: HarperPerennial, 1993.

Blood Sugar and/or Hypoglycemia

Airola, Paavo. *Hypoglycemia: A Better Approach*. Phoenix, AZ: Health Plus Publishers, 1977.

Appleton, Nancy. *Lick the Sugar Habit*. New York, NY: Avery, 1996.

———. *Lick the Sugar Habit Sugar Counter*. New York, NY: Avery, 2001.

Brand-Miller, Jeannie, Thomas Wolever, Stephen Colagiuri, and Kaye Foster-Powell. *The Glucose Revolution: The Authoritative Guide to the Glycemic Index*. New York, NY: Marlowe & Company, 1999.

DesMaisons, Kathleen. *Potatoes Not Prozac*. New York, NY: Simon & Schuster, 1998.

Heller, Richard F., and Rachael F. Heller. *The Carbohydrate Addict's Lifespan Program*. New York, NY: Penguin Putnam, Inc., 1997.

Carbohydrate/Protein

Braly, James, and Ron Hoggan. *Dangerous Grains*. New York, NY: Avery, 2002.

Eades, Michael, and Mary Dan Eades. *Protein Power*. New York, NY: 1996.

Gottschall, Elaine. *Breaking the Vicious Cycle*. Kirkton, ON: Kirkton Press, 1994.

Sears, Barry. *Enter The Zone*. New York, NY: Regan Books, 1995.

Digestion and Enzymes

Cichoke, Anthony. *The Complete Book of Enzyme Therapy*. Garden City Park, NY: Avery, 1999.

Howell, Edward. *Food Enzymes for Health & Longevity*. Twin Lakes, WI: Lotus Press, 1994.

Food-Related

Scheer, James, Lynn Allison, and Charlie Fox. *The Garlic Cure*. Fargo, ND: Alpha Omega Press, 2002.

Syndrome X

Challem, Jack, Berton Berkson, and Melissa Diane Smith. *Syndrome X: The*

Complete Nutritional Program to Prevent and Reverse Insulin Resistance. New York, NY: John Wiley & Sons, 2000.

Romaine, Deborah, and Jennifer Marks. *Syndrome X: Managing Insulin Resistance.* New York, NY: HarperTorch, 2000.

Yeast

Crook, William. *Nature's Own Candida Cure.* Vancouver, BC: Alive Books, 2000.

Martin, Jeanne Marie, and Zoltan Rona. *Complete Candida Yeast Guidebook.* Roseville, CA: Prima Publishing, 2000.

Vitamins and Other Nutrients

Balch, Phyllis A. *Prescription for Herbal Healing.* New York, NY: Avery, 2002.

Balch, Phyllis A., and James Balch. *Prescription for Nutritional Healing.* New York, NY: Avery, 2000.

Baldinger, Kathleen. *The World's Oldest Health Plan.* Lancaster, PA: Starburst Publishing, 1994.

Challem, Jack, and Melissa Diane Smith. *Basic Health Publications User's Guide to Vitamin E.* North Bergen, NJ: Basic Health Publications, 2002.

D'Adamo, Peter. *Eat Right for Your Type.* New York, NY: G.P. Putnam's Sons, 1996.

Davis, Adelle. *Let's Get Well.* New York, NY: Harcourt Brace Jovanovich, 1965.

———. *Let's Eat Right to Keep Fit.* New York, NY: Harcourt Brace Jovanovich, 1970.

Lieberman, Sheri, and Nancy Bruning. *The Real Vitamin & Mineral Book.* Garden City Park, NY: Avery, 1990.

Lininger, Skye, Jonathan Wright, Steve Austin, et al. *The Natural Pharmacy.* Rocklin, CA: Prima Publishing, 1998.

Murray, Michael, and Joseph Pizzorno. *Encyclopedia of Natural Medicine.* Rocklin, CA: Prima Publishing, 1998.

Smith, Melissa Diane. *Basic Health Publications User's Guide to Chromium.* North Bergen, NJ: Basic Health Publications, 2002.

Zucker, Martin. *Basic Health Publications User's Guide to Coenzyme Q_{10}.* North Bergen, NJ: Basic Health Publications, 2002.

General

Khalsa, Dharma Singh. *Brain Longevity.* New York, NY: Warner Books, 1997.

Lipton, Bruce. *The Biology of Belief: Unleashing the Power of Consciousness, Matter, and Miracles.* Santa Rosa, CA: Mountain of Love/Elite Books, 2005.

Schwartz, George. *In Bad Taste: The MSG Syndrome.* Santa Fe, NM: Health Press, 1988.

Sears, Barry. *Omega Rx Zone: The Miracle of the New High-Dose Fish Oil.* New York, NY: Regan Books, 2002.

Wiley, T.S. *Lights Out: Sleep, Sugar, and Survival.* New York, NY: Pocket Books, 2000.

Index

About the
Author

Kathleen O'Bannon, C.N.C., is the author of six books on nutrition and natural foods cooking. Her articles and recipes have been published in magazines, including *Alive Magazine, Canada's Healthy Living Guide, Energy Times,* and *Nature's Impact,* and in newspapers, including, *The Toronto Globe and Mail, The Register-Guard* (Eugene, Oregon), *The Stouffville Tribune, The Toronto Star, The Toronto Sun,* and the *Uxbridge Times-Journal.* Kathleen is an international speaker, lecturer, and seminar leader who has taught nutrition, natural foods cooking, and natural cosmetics in the United States and Canada. She has appeared on more than 5,000 radio and TV shows in both Canada and the United States, including *Canada AM,* CBC-Radio's *The 4 to 6 Show, 100 Huntley Street, The Joy Show, Praise the Lord, The 700 Club, Toronto Today,* and her own show, *Living Naturally.* At Kathleen's Cooking and Nutrition Centre in Toronto, Ontario, she taught natural foods and vegetarian cooking and offered classes in nutrition and yoga.

Kathleen is currently working on several humanitarian projects devoted to helping with the HIV/AIDS pandemic in Africa; one project involves a custom-designed functional food. Some of the royalties from this book will go toward supporting her humanitarian work.

Kathleen collects carrots of every kind and has about 300 different cups, sculptures, plates, jewelry, figurines, oil paintings, pen-and-ink drawings, and magnets all with carrots as the main theme—hence her nickname, the Carrot Lady. She is also an avid hiker, mountain biker, and rock collector. She can be reached at www.healthaliveproducts.com.